# CROSS-CURRENTS
# IN EUROPEAN LITERATURE

## PUBLICATIONS OF THE DEPARTMENT OF ITALIAN
## UNIVERSITY COLLEGE, DUBLIN

General Editor: John C. Barnes

Concetto La Malfa, *Ricordi di Sicilia: cinque racconti*
Concetto La Malfa, *Sicilia nel cuore: racconti e poesie*
Concetto La Malfa, *Stanze in famiglia: commedia in quattro scene*, with an English translation by Mary Casey
Concetto La Malfa, *Una macchia nel sole*, with an English translation by Cormac Ó Cuilleanáin
Renzo Ricchi, *Five One-act Plays*, introduced and translated by Renzo D'Agnillo
S. F. Boyd and others, *Cross-currents in European Literature*

*Stephen F. Boyd*  *Marella Buckley*
*Patricia Coughlan*  *Christopher P. Gaynor*
*Caoimhín Mac Giolla Léith*  *Catherine O'Brien*
*J. Henry O'Shea*  *Robert Pickering*
*Hugh Prior*  *Hilda Smyth*

# CROSS-CURRENTS IN EUROPEAN LITERATURE

DUBLIN
UCD DEPARTMENT OF ITALIAN

1996

Printed and bound by ColourBooks Ltd, Dublin, Ireland

First published 1996

by

Department of Italian
University College
Dublin 4
Ireland

A catalogue record for this book is available from the British Library.

ISBN  1 898473 52 8

Cover design by Jarlath Hayes

# PREFACE

These papers were presented at the first literary conference organized by the School of Language and Literature, University College, Cork. The strategic purpose of the conference, which took place in February 1992, was to draw attention to the fact that the UCC Language Departments were not concerned solely with language teaching but derived much of their vitality from literary research. The conference's scholarly objective was to highlight the influence and impact which different literary traditions have had and continue to have on each other. The conference is now an annual event and continues to investigate themes related to the idea of cross-currents.

Of the contributors, Henry O'Shea belongs to the community of Glenstal Abbey, County Limerick, while two others are members of University College, Dublin: Caoimhín Mac Giolla Léith, a lecturer in the Department of Modern Irish, and Hugh Prior, a doctoral student and part-time tutor in the Department of Italian. The remaining writers are all members of UCC. Marella Buckley and Hilda Smith are postgraduate students in, respectively, the departments of French and German, while the following departments are represented by members of their staffs: Classics (Christopher Gaynor), English (Patricia Coughlan), French (Robert Pickering), Italian (Catherine O'Brien) and Spanish (Stephen Boyd).

Publication of this volume has been made possible by subscriptions from the Departments of Ancient Classics, English, French, German, Irish, Italian and Spanish, as well as by a grant from UCC's Arts Faculty Research Fund. This support is acknowledged with gratitude. Thanks are also due to John Barnes of the Department of Italian in University College, Dublin for accepting this publication.

# CONTENTS

# ET IN ARCADIA EGO:
# THE PASTORAL LAMENT AND
# THE EUROPEAN LITERARY TRADITION

## Christopher P. Gaynor

It could be claimed that the fountain Arethusa, the legendary source of inspiration of pastoral poetry, has produced a most fruitful stream of cross-currents in European literature.

As the title of this essay I have preferred the version "Et in Arcadia ego" to the alternative "Et ego in Arcadia." The former, which is the original, coined at some time in the Renaissance, means "Even in Arcadia, I [Death] am to be found." The latter form is usually taken (by Goethe, Schiller and Nietzsche, among others) to mean "I too have been in Arcadia."[1] This version is used as the title of the first chapter of *Brideshead Revisited*, where the Oxford of the Twenties is equated with the idyllic life of Arcadia.

Poussin's painting entitled *Et in Arcadia Ego* expresses visually the essential character and mood of the pastoral lament. E. H. Gombrich describes it as follows:

> It shows a calm, sunny southern landscape. Beautiful young men and a fair and dignified young woman have gathered round a large tomb of stone. One of the shepherds—for shepherds they are, as we see by their wreaths and their shepherds' staffs—has knelt down to try to decipher the inscription on the tomb and a second one points towards it while he looks at the fair shepherdess who, like her companion opposite, stands in silent melancholy. It is inscribed in Latin and it says ET IN ARCADIA EGO (Even in Arcady I am): I, Death, reign even in the idyllic dreamland of the pastorals, in Arcady.[2]

It was the Greek poet Theocritus (third century BC) who founded pastoral poetry as a genre and invented the pastoral lament. He first introduced into literature the pleasance, or *locus amoenus*, the backdrop for the drama of the pastoral. It is generally a set piece with trees, shade, a seat and a fountain; here shepherds meet in the midday heat and engage in pastoral songs about love, other human emotions and even death. Theocritus usually sets the scene of the pastoral in Sicily, his native land. Pastoral poetry is normally nostalgic or escapist in character; it found its first favour in the large city of Alexandria, among Greeks who longed for their more rustic homeland, and has been practised mainly in cities and courts ever since. Theocritus constructed a simple pleasance into which his readers, or listeners, could escape from the complexities of urban life and experience the simple emotions of shepherds in a Golden Age. Vergil extended this pleasance; it now became a whole countryside, Arcadia—not the real Arcadia of Southern Greece, but a spiritual landscape.[3]

As E. Lambert has put it, the pastoral lament basically consists of "placing sorrow" in the pleasance, or in Arcadia, where, untrammelled by the complexities of everyday urban life, the sorrow, or sense of loss, may be expressed and worked through in a sympathetic environment, and mitigated and gradually absorbed by the inherently healing power of nature.[4] And according to P. M. Sachs the pastoral lament is, in form and in content, a ritualistic or structured working-through (in Freudian terms), or catharsis (in Aristotelian terms) of grief.[5] It owes much of its inspiration to traditional laments for the Vegetation-god.[6] Man may externalize, or express, his emotional reaction to death in this controlled ritualistic form, and may hope that both he himself and the dead object of his lament will somehow share in the assured resurrection of the Vegetation-god in the spring. The many conventions and figures of the traditional pastoral lament are intended to express grief in a ritual fashion; repetitions, refrains, reiterated questions (such as "Where were ye, Nymphs?"), the sympathetic mourning of nature, the strewing of flowers, the procession of mourners, are all part of a controlled grieving process. Some are intended to express grief verbally, some to distance the mourner from the dead, and some, such as calls on Nature to mourn, are there to cultivate the illusion that man has power over Nature.

It is useful to examine examples of the traditional pastoral lament, ranging from antiquity to products of post-Renaissance English literature, such as Milton's *Lycidas*, Shelley's *Adonais* and Arnold's *Thyrsis*. I feel that the course followed by the pastoral lament in English is paradigmatic of European literature in general. My main point of focus is the stance of the individual poet in relation to the genre's traditional norms. I shall take the inherited conventions and figures for granted and not comment on them unless there is some unusual treatment of them. Three aspects of the pastoral lament deserve particular attention: the pastoral pleasance in which the poet "places his sorrow"; the self-consciousness of the poet in the act of composing his poem; the means of solace which may be found at the end of the poem.

In the prototype of the species, Theocritus's *Lament for Daphnis*, the lament proper is set within a frame consisting of a highly poetic dialogue between a shepherd and a goatherd, who verbally conjure up the pastoral landscape in which the sorrow will be placed. Even though this is the prototype, the modes of expressing or working through grief are conventional. There is no final solace within the lament itself; the solace is derived from the power of the pleasant landscape, conjured up in the frame, to absorb and dissipate sorrow.

The second example of the genre that we have from antiquity, Bion's *Lament for Adonis*, is basically a lament for a Nature-god. Since the subject is a Nature-god we may regard the pastoral landscape as given. In his composition the poet focuses on the grieving of Aphrodite for her dead lover. Bion himself, like his predecessor Theocritus, maintains the unobtrusiveness of an epic poet. The final solace is derived from the fact that Adonis is palpably a Nature-god who will rise again. It could be claimed that, given these circumstances, the *Lament for Adonis* is not a pastoral lament in the strict sense of the term. Even so, Shelley in his *Adonais* uses this poem as the basic framework and sustaining material of his lament for Keats.

In the third example of the genre, Moschus's *Lament for Bion*, new ground was broken: Bion was a real person, who as a writer of pastoral poetry could be allowed into Arcadia by proxy. This innovation soon became a standard convention in the pastoral lament. Another novel feature of this poem is the first-person presence of the poet, who contributes in his own name to the grieving process described. Although the figures and conventions of grieving are the usual ones, the process is undermined by the poet's realization that, while nature will revive in spring, we humans will remain dead. He has to seek solace in his faith in the power of poetry; perhaps, like Orpheus, he could descend to Hades, enthral the

Sicilian Persephone with Sicilian pastorals and restore Bion to his hills. It was this final section of the poem which provided inspiration for Matthew Arnold's *Thyrsis*.

Vergil's *Eclogues* were to exercise the most enduring influence on subsequent pastoral poets, and it was Vergil who established Arcadia as a landscape of the spirit. To a greater degree than earlier poets, he introduced contemporary people and events into the pastoral world, and in his fifth eclogue he offers the ultimate solace when the dead Daphnis transcends death and enters heaven.[7] Two other characteristics of the Vergilian pastoral that were to influence later poets were an increasing presence and self-consciousness of the poet and a pervading sense of nostalgia, generated by his awareness of the fragility of the pastoral world, under relentless threat of destruction by a harsh, brutal outside world, usually centred on the city.[8]

The pastoral appeared tentatively in the Middle Ages whenever a minor precursor of the Renaissance arose. It returned with renewed splendour with the Renaissance proper. It was first revived at the humanistic courts of Italy, then spread to Spain, France, England and somewhat later to Germany, where it acted as a means of escape from the horrors of the Thirty Years War.

Milton's *Lycidas* is a work in the mainstream of pastoral literature as it developed during the Renaissance. The poet no longer has to invent his landscape but he does introduce aspects of the British countryside into the pastoral.[9] In the procession of mourners—a long-established convention of the pastoral lament—St Peter appears by virtue of his role as pastor (this role of his in the pastoral world was well established in the Renaissance period) and comments in pastoral terminology on the ills of the church. The poet's self-awareness is much to the fore. Milton, while reflecting on Lycidas's short life, has doubts about his own devotion to poetry, but these are resolved by the end.[10] The poem transcends the pagan elements of the pastoral from which it progresses, while the poet's final solace comes from his belief in the Christian doctrine of the Resurrection.

In the eighteenth century the pastoral became over-formal and stereotyped while the conventions grew thin and hollow from over-use—an extreme case of intertextuality losing contact with anything outside itself. It then seemed that Romanticism, with its interest in the immediate experience of nature, had drawn the final curtain on the pastoral. Shelley's *Adonais*, however, a lament for Keats cast in pastoral form, is a great *tour de force*. At the start, though with variations and elaborations, it closely follows Bion's *Lament for Adonis*. The mother summoned to mourn her poet-son, however, is now not Aphrodite but Urania, the muse of astronomy. Death, usually a rather shadowy figure (embodied in Bion's poem in the person of Pluto in the Underworld), is here depicted as a really terrifying presence, in the best Gothic tradition, like a character from a modern horror-film. The imagery is that of Shelley at his best: the procession of mourners is made up not of persons but of personifications of the emotions and fantasies that inspired Keats's poetry. In spite of the risk he runs, Shelley manages to avoid banality and frigidity, using his source in an inventive manner. Just as Bion, according to Moschus, was poisoned, so Keats, according to Shelley, was driven to death by a hostile reviewer. As the poem progresses, Shelley identifies more and more with the trials and tribulations of the dead Keats, while the final solace comes from a belief, inspired by neo-Platonism, in the soul's ultimate return to the Kingdom of Light.

The Victorian poet Matthew Arnold, in his *Thyrsis*, is patently obvious and self-aware in his efforts to generate a pastoral lament for his dead friend Clough. After the Romantics, Arcadia could no longer be regarded as given. Arnold begins by depicting the country-side around Oxford in the realistic manner of a lesser Romantic. He tentatively identifies individual pastoral elements in the actual land-scape, and for a passing moment can in Vergilian manner identify the actual countryside with Arcadia and transform the mode of his poem into a pastoral lament. Interspersed with his description of the actual countryside and the memories it evokes for him are sporadic pastoral phrases and references such as "my pipe is lost" or "my shepherd's holiday", and the poet gives himself the pastoral name Corydon, while Clough is Thyrsis. Finally, a detailed evocation of the floral exuberance of high summer, reminiscent of the flower motifs of the pastoral lament, seems to be the cue for the poem to expand into a fully fledged pastoral. The poet and Clough are now really Corydon and Thyrsis, and Arnold takes up a theme from the *Lament for Bion*—perhaps he could win back the dead poet from the Underworld by charming Pluto's wife Persephone with some Sicilian pastoral strain:

> She loved the Dorian pipe, the Dorian strain.
> But ah, of our poor Thames she never heard!
> Her foot the Cumner cowslips never stirr'd!
> And we should tease her with our plaint in vain.

Unable to sustain the pastoral mode, Arnold returns to the actual countryside around Oxford for its solacing effect.

The fountain Arethusa finally oozed into the mud of Flanders, and even Yeats's attempt to mourn Robert Gregory in a pastoral lament is generally regarded as not very felicitous. For the post-war Modernists, such as Eliot in *The Waste Land*, "the nymphs are departed."

## NOTES

1    See G. Highet, *The Classical Tradition: Greek and Roman Influences on Western Literature* [1949] (Oxford, Clarendon Press, 1951), p. 614, additional note.

2    E. H. Gombrich, *The Story of Art* (Oxford, Phaidon, 1972), p. 308.

3    See B. Snell, "Arcadia: The Discovery of a Spiritual Landscape", in *The Discovery of the Mind: The Greek Origins of European Thought*, translated by T. G. Rosenmeyer (Oxford, Blackwell, 1953), pp. 281–309.

4    E. Lambert, *Placing Sorrow: A Study of the Pastoral Elegy from Theocritus to Milton* (Chapel Hill, North Carolina, University of North Carolina Press, 1976), pp. xiii ff.

5    P. M. Sachs, *The English Elegy: Studies in the Genre from Spencer to Yeats*. (Baltimore–London, Johns Hopkins University Press, 1985), pp. 18ff.

6    One of these conventions, the procession of the mourners, which first appears in Theocritus's *Lament for Daphnis*, seems in this instance to owe its inspiration to Aeschylus's *Prometheus Bound*; but it may be that the structure of the tragedy itself is based on a traditional lament.

7    Understandably this theme of resurrection became common as a source of solace in pastorals of the Christian era.

8    See L. Lerner, "The Eclogues and the Pastoral Tradition", in *Vergil and his Influence: Bimillenial Studies*, edited by C. Martindale (Bristol, Bristol Classical Press, 1984), pp. 195ff.

9    E.g. "Mona" and "Deva" in the "Where were ye, Nymphs [...]?" section.

10   See P. M. Sachs, *The English Elegy*, pp. 104ff, p. 116.

# FROM FIONN MacCUMHAILL
# TO MELCHIORRE CESAROTTI

## Catherine O'Brien

Ossian, sublimest, simplest bard of all
Whom English infidels Macpherson call.[1]

These lines by the critic G. F. Black help to highlight in a striking way
the controversy that has always surrounded the poems of Ossian by
the Scottish writer James Macpherson (1736–96),[2] which made an
eventful entry onto the English literary scene in June 1760 and
subsequently played a decisive part in the development of pre-
Romantic literature throughout Europe.[3] In England and elsewhere
a heated debate immediately took place with Ossian and Macpherson
at its centre. Were Macpherson's poems authentic translations or
were they just a clever modern recreation by someone who insisted
that they were genuine so that he could contribute to the fashion of
the time, which valued and appreciated anything that was primitive
and old?

When Macpherson subsequently presented *Fingal* (1762) and
*Temora* (1763) as translations of lost epic poems composed by Ossian
in the third century AD that had been transmitted orally for fifteen
centuries,[4] the translator's honesty was again challenged, and the
question of the authenticity of these poems raged on for many years.
Hugh Blair, the literary dictator of Scotland, placed Ossian above
Homer while Samuel Johnson, who held sway in England, declared
Macpherson a cheat and refused to recognize any literary merit in his
translations. Macpherson was well prepared for this challenge. In
order to place Ossian in a historical context and explain the customs
of Ossian's era he included learned essays in each edition of his
poems; but still the suspicions would not go away. While the English
doubted that their Scottish antagonists could produce authentic

originals, the anger of the Irish knew no bounds and they accused Macpherson of having stolen their national heroes. Macpherson was aware of the existence of Ossianic poetry in Ireland but condemned it as spurious. One of the most cogent arguments used by the Irish against Macpherson was that he had confused the protagonists of the poetic cycles of primitive Irish poetry—something, they argued, which would not have happened had Macpherson used genuine Gaelic originals. The commonly accepted judgement on Macpherson is that of the Highland Society of Scotland, which, following intensive investigations, came to the conclusion in 1805 that Macpherson's poems were not translations but very free elaborations of Gaelic legends. Macpherson always denied this allegation, but, although he did have some genuine fragments of ancient poetry in his possession, he never produced any significant original texts and it is generally believed that the poems were ingenious inventions by Macpherson.[5] What he did achieve through his poetry, however, was to highlight the wandering, sensitive and melancholic spirit of the Celt while at the same time providing a rich source of poetic inspiration which had a major impact on pre-Romantic and Romantic literature in Europe.

When the Ossianic poems appeared, many readers outside the British Isles were not particularly concerned about their authenticity. What mattered more was that the poems of Ossian made a dramatic entry onto the literary scene just when throughout Europe there was a passionate interest in poetry that was close to nature, full of deep feeling and the work of an ancient poet. Macpherson's poems were successful because they appeared to be the poetic testimony of an ancient poet. This new European taste was also fostered by the work of Paul Henri Mallet on the mythology of the northern European countries and by the melancholic poetry of Edward Young and Thomas Gray.[6]

In many ways the Ossianic poems are similar to the works of these writers: although the background is almost always war, the descriptions of battles are cold, vague and artificial and are there solely to highlight the valour, courage, generosity, heroism and passion of the warriors. Readers were struck by features such as lake landscapes, cloud-covered mountains, grey skies, green seas, storms, mists, ruins and the bitter-sweet appearance of the stars, which often symbolized the tragic end of love affairs, the futility of hopes and dreams, or the longing for past ages. The language played its part too: Macpherson's prose was energetic, passionate, picturesque and full of rhythm. Extensive use was made of periphrasis, apostrophe, and adjectives and metaphors suited to the deep melancholy and sentimentality which envelop the works and appealed so strongly to contemporary readers.

The poems of Ossian met with instant success in France and Germany: the first partial translation of Macpherson's Ossian appeared in France (the translator was Le Tourneur), while Germany was the country that produced the greatest number of translations.[7] Whereas the early French and German translations were of individual poems from the 1760 *Fragments*, Italy was immediately presented with a complete translation of these Celtic poems. This was due to Melchiorre Cesarotti (1730–1804), Professor of Greek and Hebrew at the University of Padua. Cesarotti lived in Venice from 1760 to 1768, and there he met Charles Sackville, who had received the first volume of fragments of Ossian's poetry from England and introduced Cesarotti to this poetry towards the end of 1762.[8] Immediately struck by this new phenomenon, Cesarotti decided to learn English at once so that he could translate Ossian into Italian. He mastered English in the space of six months and produced the first complete translation of Macpherson's *Fingal* in 1763. He later translated *Temora* and other Ossianic poems as they were published by Macpherson.[9] Despite attempts by Italian rivals to outdo him, Cesarotti's translations remained the most popular in Italy. The various editions sold out immediately and there were many reprints, the last edition by the translator being published in Pisa in 1801. In this Cesarotti revised his version by comparing it once more with the English text and with the French translation by Le Tourneur. He made changes to emphasize the author's Celtic character, while the translation was accompanied by numerous quotations explaining how he had translated and why he had made certain choices.

The success of these Ossianic poems in Italy was also largely due to the fact that at the time of their appearance many felt that literature should be moving in new directions. This trend was being hotly debated in Italian literary circles, with primitive and nature poetry being much praised. Cesarotti, with his translations of the Celtic bard, revealed new possibilities and thereby ushered in the era of pre-Romanticism, which made the decisive move away from the culture of the Enlightenment and opened the way for Romanticism. Ossian filled a gap and provided a new world of poetry that was free from the artificiality and cloying musicality of the Arcadian movement. Walter

Binni assesses the value of Cesarotti's Ossian not so much in terms of the poetry itself as of the poetic material which opened up new horizons that could be exploited by the sensitivity and creativity of Italians.[10]

Cesarotti had seen that the desire for something new was answered by Ossian's anxious, melancholic atmosphere. With their overpowering cultivation of melancholic visions, the Ossianic poems—both in the original English and especially in translation—became fundamental texts in Italian pre-Romanticism. In due course the Romantics adopted many of Ossian's poetic themes: the silence of deserted tombs, funeral elegies, the isolated beauty of human life, the mystery of nature and of its isolation.

We have the first idea of Cesarotti's attitude towards Ossian in a letter he wrote to Macpherson in 1762. He praised Macpherson for the felicitous discovery of the Ossian poems, which had so enriched literature: "I am filled with enthusiasm for your Ossian. Morven has become my Parnassus and Lora my Hippocrene. I dream constantly of your heroes."[11] Cesarotti also remarked that Ossian demonstrates both the superiority and the weaknesses of ancient poetry. "Scotland," he wrote, "has presented a Homer who neither yawns nor babbles, is never vulgar or long-winded, whose poetry is simple, fast, precise, balanced and varied."[12] He considered Ossian superior to Homer in that he avoided the Greek poet's harshness and incongruities while maintaining those qualities of equilibrium and balance deemed essential in a work of art by the classicist rationalist movement. In the same letter he referred to the authenticity question but was unconcerned by its implications. He accepted Macpherson's explanations and said that were he to discover that Macpherson and not Ossian were the author it would not matter because "Ossian's style is old regardless of whether Ossian is ancient or not."[13] Cesarotti was later honoured by the Royal Irish Academy for his work on Ossian, but in his letter of acceptance he again passed over the question of the poems' authenticity and focused on their excellence, which he said had made "the name of the green Erin and the wooden Morven dear to all literary enthusiasts in Europe".[14]

It is, however, in his treatise on tragedy and particularly in his essay on the origin and progress of poetry that we find the true genesis of Cesarotti's Ossian.[15] These works allowed him to participate in the debate which expressed Italy's yearning for a live and modern kind of literature. Cesarotti exploited rationalist principles to criticize the

false rules of academic classicism, Enlightenment ideas to establish
the need for poetry that can educate, and pre-Romantic motives to
vouch for the originality and individuality of the poet and the
fantastic element in poetry. Ossian was what he needed to prove his
points.

In his espousal of the new literary phenomenon Cesarotti
discovered that he had much in common with the Celtic bard. His
enthusiasm, together with his delight in primitive poetry, is reflected
in the explanatory notes accompanying his translations. He expressed his admiration by frequently comparing Ossian with ancient
and modern poets, and this is one of the more interesting aspects of
his observations. When praising Ossian's poetic method he notes:
"In the presentation of the hero of a poem one of the basic rules is that
the first impression given to the reader should be a favourable one
[...]. Nobody executed this method better than Ossian."[16] He quotes
a modern poet who held that the poet's art, if considered from a
descriptive point of view, should highlight action that is capable of
striking several chords at the same time. If this is so, says Cesarotti,
then Ossian must be judged as a poet *par excellence*. He observes that
similes are common to Ossian and other ancient poets but that no
one used them more beautifully than the Celtic poet.[17]

In short, Cesarotti saw Ossian as superior to all other ancient
poets because he considered him more refined in sentiment and
expression and therefore closer to what the eighteenth century
appreciated in poetry. When he assesses the character of the Celtic
heroes Cesarotti's observations are often sharp and to the point. He
sees Fingal as a passionate hero who is neither hard nor coarse, full
of humanity and tolerance, while, from the point of view of literary
taste, the reader is left with the clear impression that Cesarotti found
in this poetry of nature and sentiment something that fulfilled the
prevalent desire for ethical and artistic refinement.

What is striking in Cesarotti's observations is the frequent
comparison between Ossian and Homer, which almost always
favours Ossian. This was in effect a reflection of the debate between
classicists and modernists: the former held that beauty and perfection could be found only in the imitation of classical authors, while
the modernists disagreed. Cesarotti fought his personal battle principally in his notes and critical observations on the Ossian poems. He
thought it vital that classical poetry be challenged, especially in
Venetia, where people were by and large fanatical supporters of the

classical authors. Cesarotti saw that such fanaticism was having a negative effect on literature as it denied that change was possible or that sources other than Greek and Roman ones could be valid. Cesarotti's comparison of Ossian to Homer was therefore deliberately intended to teach young and unbiased people that Homer was not the only source of poetic inspiration. By comparing Homer with another poet whose circumstances were similar, he wished to show how the Greek poet could have achieved greater perfection and that his example should not always be cited as law. This was the driving spirit behind his critical observations accompanying the Ossian poems. In his theoretical work *On the Origin and Progress of Poetic Art* Cesarotti reflected on the extreme situations that can be produced by literary rules: "The most recent prejudice in poetry states that since Homer wrote the *Iliad* all rules relating to an epic poem must be taken from him. How many critics in the past and how many still maintain that Milton is not an epic poet simply because Adam is not Achilles and *Paradise Lost* is not the siege of Troy?"[18]

In his letter to Macpherson Cesarotti regretted the fact that many classical Italian critics condemned Ossian simply because he had not read Aristotle's *Poetics* and because his name could not be declined in either Greek or Latin. Unless modern authors borrowed from the ancients, he wrote, those critics would not recognize any merit in their work. They also denied that the Ossian poems had poetic merit because they believed Ossian to be a modern fabrication. Cesarotti, however, used Ossian to criticize Homer and to prove that beauty and perfection were not the exclusive preserve of ancient Greek writers. Much of the controversy surrounding Ossian in Italy centred on Cesarotti's praise of the Celtic bard and demotion of Homer. The attempt by Cesarotti's opponents to prove that the Ossian poems were inauthentic was thus a strategy designed to invalidate the comparison with Homer.

Cesarotti faced many difficulties in translating the peculiar characteristics of the Ossianic texts encountered in Macpherson's melodic prose. A literal Italian prose translation, he wrote, would have made the reader aware of the difficulties he faced. But he compounded the difficulties by opting to translate into Italian verse. In his translations Cesarotti decided to remain faithful to Ossian's spirit rather than making a literal translation. At the same time he attempted to establish a distance between the translator and the original author. He changed the names and Italianized them because their original forms would not fit into the harmony of the Italian verse. He felt the need to explain and justify his changes and innovations. His notes on the following lines exemplify this:

> Allor d'Erina
> il generoso duce il suo leggiadro
> spirito ripigliò.[19]

[Then the strong Irish leader summoned up his fine spirit.]

Cesarotti refers to the English text ("powerful spirit", of which a literal translation would be "possente spirito"), but justifies his selection of "leggiadro" by observing that this adjective has a greater sense of gentleness and nobility and that these were the dominant characteristics of Cuchulainn, the hero referred to in these lines. He also claims that the French translator missed this point in translating "sa grande âme".[20]

More important than the images and expressions is the rhythm of Cesarotti's versification. Seeking a metre that would retain Macpherson's rhythmic originality, he chose the hendecasyllable for the freedom it would give him to translate the unusual sounds and primitive tones inherent in Macpherson's prose; and he dispensed with rhyme in order to give himself still greater freedom and precision. His blank verse acquires new strength and musicality from the use of exclamations, interrogations, alliteration, *enjambement* and mid-line pauses.

This work by Cesarotti paved the way for many outstanding literary figures in Italy around the turn of the eighteenth century. Vittorio Alfieri based his hendecasyllables on Cesarotti's and also drew heavily on the melancholic northern landscapes which Cesarotti favoured. *Il bardo della Selva Nera* ("The Bard of the Dark Wood"), written by Vincenzo Monti in 1806, was directly inspired by the characters and stories of Cesarotti's Ossian, while it also highlights the feats of a great contemporary hero, Napoleon Bonaparte.

At the beginning of the nineteenth century the neo-classical literary movement reached its maturity in the work of Ugo Foscolo. For many Romantic poets the beauty found in classical writers was supreme and Homer represented everything that was immortal and eternal in poetry. This neo-classicism developed principally in Padua, where Cesarotti, translator of Homer as well as Ossian, taught and where Foscolo was his pupil. It was after Cesarotti's decisive intervention in the field of poetry that pre-Romantic culture was ready to accept the work of poets such as Alfieri, Monti, Foscolo and Leopardi.

Foscolo's poetry is strongly influenced by many Ossianic themes: the fleeting nature of human things, the function of the tomb in linking the present with the memory of famous people and their deeds, the importance of the poet in keeping the memory of the dead alive in poetry—these are all key themes in Foscolo's poetry and were certainly brought to his attention in Padua by Cesarotti. Giacomo Leopardi, the greatest of the Italian Romantic poets, acknowledged the influence of Homer, Virgil, Petrarch and Ossian on his poetic formation. There are many parallels between his work and that of Ossian, Macpherson and Cesarotti. His "Canzone all'Italia" ["Song to Italy"] praises the poet Simonides for keeping alive the memory of the three hundred men who died in the Battle of Thermopylae, and thus parallels the theme of Ossian keeping alive the memory of his dead friends and companions. Many of the anxious questions asked in Leopardi's poetry recall those of Ossian—questions that are not always answered, though the silence surrounding them is often starker and more chilling in Leopardi than in Ossian.

It is clear that Ossianic poetry was a watershed that introduced readers to a different poetic world with exciting new metrical, lyrical and linguistic values. With his Ossian Cesarotti concentrated on the desire for melancholy, with nature a reflection of man's grief and the instincts and impulses of the men of Ossian's time enveloped in an aura of sentimentality. But this also marks the limit of Cesarotti's pre-Romanticism and explains the subsequent decline of the Ossianic vogue in Italy. After 1815 Italians found greater sustenance in the noble strength of Alfieri's tragedies, which took a stand against tyranny, and in the poetry of Foscolo, which was permeated with patriotism. Ossian's sentimental, melancholic tones had to give way to poetry which engaged with the political realities of early nineteenth-century Italy. That step forward, however, would not have been achieved if Cesarotti had not first freed Italian literature from the artificiality and aridity of Arcadia and prepared the ground for the heightened awareness of Romantic sensitivity.

# NOTES

1   G. F. Black, "Macpherson's Ossian and the Ossianic Controversy: A Contribution towards a Biography", *Bulletin of New York Public Library*, xxx (1926), p. 7.

2   James Macpherson, *Fragments of Ancient Poetry, Collected in the Highlands of Scotland, and Translated from the Galic [sic] or Erse Language* (Edinburgh, Hamilton and Balfour, 1760).

3   The Ossianic vogue lasted from 1760 to the mid-nineteenth century; see E. D. Snyder, *The Celtic Revival in English Literature* (Gloucester, Mass., Peter Smith, 1965), pp. 69–192.

4   *Fingal, an Ancient Epic Poem, in Eight Books, together with Several Other Poems; Composed by Ossian, the Son of Fingal; Translated from the Galic Language by James Macpherson* (London, Becket and Dehondt, 1762); *Temora, an Ancient Epic Poem, in Eight Books, together with Several Other Poems, translated from the Galic Language by James Macpherson* (London, Becket and Dehondt, 1763).

5   See P. Van Tieghem, *Ossian en France* (Paris, Rieder, 1917), vol. i, p. 192; *Irish Sagas*, edited by M. Dillon (Cork, Mercier, 1968), p. 63.

6   Mallet's main work was on the mythology of the northern European countries, and some of the information used by Cesarotti in his explanatory notes to the poems was taken from Mallet. One of Gray's masterpieces, "Elegy Written in a Country Churchyard", was enormously successful in Europe. Cesarotti's translation of this poem appeared in 1776 and found its niche in the popularity of and demand for the so-called Ossianic poetry.

7   In 1760 two fragments which Macpherson had published earlier in the year were published in French by Turgot in the *Journal étranger*; see P. Van Tieghem, *Le Préromantisme* (Paris, Rieder, 1924), vol. i, p. 224. On Ossian in Germany see L. Marsden Price, *English Literature in Germany* (California, Ayer, 1953), vol. xxxvii, p. 124.

8   Born of an English father and a Venetian mother, Sackville lived in Venice and translated these poems word by word for Cesarotti; see G. Barbieri, *Memorie intorno alla vita ed agli studi dell'abate Cesarotti* (Pisa, Capurro, 1813), pp. 16–17.

9   *Poesie di Ossian figlio de Fingal antico poeta celtico ultimamente scoperte, e tradotte in prosa inglese da Jacopo Macpherson, e da quella trasportate in verso italiano dall'abate Melchior Cesarotti con varie annotazioni de' due traduttori* (Nice, Società Tipografica, 1780), vol. i, p. xxii.

10  W. Binni, *Melchiorre Cesarotti e il preromanticismo italiano* (Naples, ESI, 1948).

11  *Dal Muratori al Cesarotti*, edited by E. Bigi (Milan–Naples, Ricciardi, 1960), p. 486. The original copy of this letter is in the British Museum, MS. 22899 (fol. 165).

12  *Dal Muratori al Cesarotti*, p. 487.

13  *Dal Muratori al Cesarotti*, p. 488.

14  British Museum, MS. 22899, fols 361–62.

15  M. Cesarotti, *Ragionamento sopra il diletto della tragedia* (1762); *Ragionamento sopra l'origine e i progressi dell'arte poetica* (1762).

16  *Dal Muratori al Cesarotti*, p. 203.

17  *Dal Muratori al Cesarotti*, p. 204.

18  M. Cesarotti, *Sull'origine e i progressi dell'arte poetica* (1762), in *Dal Muratori al Cesarotti*, pp. 66–68.

19  *Fingal*, i. 490–92.

20  *Dal Muratori al Cesarotti*, p. 119.

# LOST FOR WORDS: LANGUAGE AND THE INFINITE IN EUROPEAN ROMANTICISM

## Robert Pickering

"Language was not powerful enough to describe the infant phenomenon":[1] so writes Dickens in *Nicholas Nickleby* (Chapter 23), confronted with the difficulties of complete expression. There is of course something disconcerting in authors who state the problematics of description only to engage subsequently in ever lengthier disquisitions on character or circumstances, particularly if the latter stand beyond normal modes of perception or experience. But the Romantic period would seem to me, after the exceptional linguistic inventiveness of European Renaissance literature and the clear emergence of a belief in the progress and general betterment of mankind (steadily affirmed in the course of the seventeenth and eighteenth centuries), to test the limits of expression, posing in a pressing way certain problems concerning language. The consequences of this pressure placed on language could be seen to influence literary currents in late nineteenth-century France, and to turn European literature in general radically away from many of the central tenets of the Romantic canon.

In a paradoxical way, the outward and visible sign of the problems with language experienced by the early nineteenth century frequently takes the form of facility of description, rather than that of language's shortfall. In Dickens precisely, as in other European authors who sometimes seem to push description to excessive lengths—Balzac (1799–1850) or Manzoni (1785–1873)—, it might be legitimate to view prolixity as a form of compensation, counterbalancing the inner, intractable core of perception, distanced from conventional modes of articulation, with concatenating registers of description which home in on virtualities of psychology or even social relationships, and prepare the way for what would otherwise appear to be unexplained or illogical changes in behaviour and thought.

This is not, of course, systematically the case. In Manzoni's *I promessi sposi* ("The Betrothed")—that great historical novel published in 1827 at the height of the Romantic triumph on a truly European scale—the claim "Who could now describe the terror and the anguish [of Lucia, the novel's heroine], who could express the innermost recesses of her soul?" comes very close to pure artifice, [2] since no sooner is it proffered than we are treated to the most precise and evocative details of the heroine's plight. Manzoni does respect a predominantly objective angle of vision for the rest of the paragraph, as if the subjective view were indeed too distressful to communicate, but an abiding impression of manipulative padding remains. At the same time, however, the dilemmas born of naming the world and experience can assume more profoundly felt connotations in the novel.

Manzoni perhaps unwittingly gives substance, by his presentation of an unnamed character, to the dialectic between, on the one hand, the inexpressible and, on the other, the structural necessity to scrutinize psychological motivation in advance of sudden apparently arbitrary oscillations by means of which alone the plot may develop. An evil warlord in strife-torn Lombardy, whose powerful influence has been built on terror before he comes into contact with the hero, Renzo, and the heroine of the novel, will turn out to be the instrument of divine Providence, assisting the lovers on their difficult way by means of a subsequent conversion which has all the trappings of an inexplicable and inconsistent about-turn. But Manzoni carefully prepares this important turning-point in the text, by situating self-identity in the context of the divine (if only in the latter's initial rejection),[3] through a lengthy series of psychological soundings. The development of the plot itself thus turns on a continuing tension between detailed examination of inner states of mind and a refusal, or an inability, to put a name to this individual of such signal and extraordinary complexity. In this light, the presence in the writing of the unnamable is far more than a structural ploy to create suspense: it centralizes and stabilizes the potential proliferation of vicissitudes in the plot, and may be linked to a recognition of the ways in which, for Manzoni, human behaviour tends at times to stand beyond circumscription in the ordinary stuff of linguistic appellation. Hence the cautious terms of Manzoni's introduction of a shadowy, larger-than-life figure, whom we feel we both know and do not know as the writing progresses: "Each time unknown or more dastardly cutthroats appeared, and on the perpetration of every notorious deed which could not immediately be ascribed to anyone in particular, people murmured the name of him whom we [...] are obliged to designate as the unnamed."[4]

The problem of full self-expression, of the acute circumscription of what is only partially apprehended as essence, particularly if it is associated with the divine, is a very ancient one. Medieval mystics such as Eckhart, Ruysbroek, St John of the Cross or St Teresa of Avila came to terms with the perception of the divine through the *via negationis*, the negative approach to the ineffable and the unspeakable which purports to define what stands beyond language by the progressive paring away of unessential concepts and characteristics. This method bit deeply into Western philosophical consciousness, and not only in the context of religious thought or contemplation: it may still be seen to be very active in the twentieth century in the work of Paul Valéry, traditionally held to be the arch-rationalist, but whose thought is now recognized as embedded solidly in early readings of the medieval mystics. For the latter, language condenses and crystallizes the divine: despite their indirectness of approach, there is no suggestion in such writers that language is ultimately inadequate in its relationship with the transcendental or the visionary.

On the surface of things, Romantic sensibility too would appear to be far removed from any misgivings concerning the representational power of language. The classic statement of a belief in the potential of words to plumb the depths of experience may be found in Victor Hugo's *Les Contemplations*. The poem "Réponse à un acte d'accusation" is explicit in its vigorous espousal of a principle of revolutionary linguistic experimentation, defending a belief that the grandiloquent and demiurgic aspirations of the Romantic mind require a breadth of language flexible enough to accommodate them:

> And against the Academy, ancient ancestor and dowageress,
> Concealing the frightened tropes under its skirts,
> And against the squared battalions of alexandrines,
> I raised a revolutionary wind.
> I placed a red bonnet on the old dictionary.[5]

In a biting, vituperative mode typical of one of Hugo's many styles, language is freed of all fossilizing and stultifying conventions. "All words now hover in complete light./Writers have liberated language": as another poem in the collection ("Ibo") states, the poet is free to scale the heights of the "visionary" or plumb the depths of the "unfathomable", in the forceful expression of a totalizing self-confidence.

If we adhere to Hugo's view, and to appraisals of the Romantic movement, language would seem to be little questioned on the grounds of its representational efficacy or adequacy. By expanding its expressive power, Hugo is attempting to harness it to the restless ambitions of Romantic sensibility—aspirations which are experiential in kind (the themes of love and of nature), rooted, therefore, in reality, but also mystical, psychological, not to mention cultural, social and political. At the most, the critical eye finds truck with Romantic indiscipline: Valéry, situating Baudelaire, adopts this approach in defining the interrelationship between the ordering, harmonizing propensities of Classicism, and the untrammelled, unstructured outpourings of Romantic sensibility ("Any form of classicism implies a preceding romanticism. [...] The essence of classicism is to come after").[6] Despite the implicit prioritization of Classicism, Valéry confirms the view of Romanticism as an intellectual and artistic period characterized by its coursing energies, one of vibrant and dynamic creativity. For the Romantic soul, the mighty thrust of eloquence in which all linguistic registers participate is seen to strip bare the depths of man's innermost motivation, to reach out for the heavens, to engage with the divine, and thus enact the general aspiration towards other-worldliness which is a very marked feature of writing of that time.

But this is only a partial view of the complexities of language and its use in the Romantic period. The huge trans-national and trans-cultural confidence is secretly undermined by attitudes to language which see in it less a source of vibrant becoming and of connection with the world, than a vehicle whose expressive powers are sometimes deeply at variance with the challenges of complete expression. In its investigative, transgressive ambitions, the Romantic mind could not but run into difficulties, as the notion of the infinite is explored in a variety of ways. Beyond its status as a constant in the thematic canon of Romanticism, the perception of the infinite tends to radicalize and polarize the writer's view of the world, thereby accentuating the ways in which the unknown, far from being apprehensible even to the seer, refuses to be encapsulated in the banal categories of conventional discourse. Coleridge (1772–1834), in his *Biographia Literaria* (1817), highlights this quest for the "beyond", praising the few transgressive minds in "speculative science" who have dared to orientate knowledge towards a "penetration to the inmost centre, from which all the lines of knowledge diverge to their ever distant circumference".[7] So too Baudelaire, later in the century, saw in Romanticism the vital expression of "modern art—which is to say, intimacy, spirituality, colour and aspiration towards the infinite".[8]

In its early stages, the perception of reality on the one hand, and the apprehension of what lies beyond it on the other, are not seen to be antithetical, and are implied to be potentially concomitant. Coleridge, outlining "the two cardinal points of poetry", urges the writer to adhere faithfully to "the truth of nature", and to tap "the power of giving the interest of novelty by the modifying colours of imagination",[9] thereby establishing the complementarity of functioning between what is recognizable, grounded in the real, and what, aided by the imagination, extends the real in infinite or "supernatural" directions. Yet this play of reality and the imagination is not always as interconnective as Coleridge himself would have it. Even in as early a work as "The Rime of the Ancyent Marinere", the return to "the firm land" of "mine own Countrée",[10] to the homely, comforting things of wedding celebrations and kirk, after the terrifying experience of the spectral and the morbid, has something to it of that same compensatory status which, I have suggested, is to be interpreted in the light of its structural function in the work of other nineteenth-century European writers. Over and above its obvious dramatic power, the play of chiaroscuro—of eery half-light and ghostly imprecision—also instils in the writing a sense of moral and eschatological antithesis, compounding the tension between highly vivid realistic details and the unearthly manifestations of the supernatural with the possibility of final salvation and absolution, achieved only in a prerequisite apocalypse of destruction.

In the emphasis placed in this poem on the paradoxical plasticity of supernatural perception (references to colouring, to tangible, perceptible entities),[11] the distance between adherence to "the truth of nature" and the free play of the imagination is at times acute, prompting a significant stanza which has nothing to it of the artificial or the rhetorical:

> O happy living things! no tongue
> Their beauty might declare:
> A spring of love gusht from my heart,
> And I bless'd them unaware!

Whether the poetic experience be "aware" or "unaware" in nature, and whatever be the precise form of the infinite—diabolical or heavenly—, the need to say, to express, to communicate is impressed upon us with an urgency which the entire text accentuates and prolongs. For the German poet Ludwig Uhland (1787–1862) the quest for the divine and the apprehension of the invisible are invested with similarly imperative connotations, as the poet comes to grips with what are perceived to be the limitations of standard forms of discourse. The "menacing voices" of the "infernal regions", the "terrifying ghosts of the night", constitute one of the polarized extremities of that dialectic between reality and the supernatural, the internal tensions of which cannot but be felt in language itself: "The mind of man, well aware that it can never apprehend the invisible, understand it with full clarity, and weary from aimless desiring, soon fixes its nostalgia on earthly images which seem to it to contain the distant glimmer of the supernatural."[12] In such a context it is poetry which is exalted, precisely in its overall expressive capacity ("Romanticism is sublime, eternal poetry, which presents in images what words cannot express, or express poorly"). This is a view which we find again in Novalis (1772–1801): given that "we are more closely bound to the invisible than to the visible", it is the task of poetry to exteriorize these intangible realms, to "express the inexpressible".[13]

To this stage, the pressure of the dialectic between the value of an earthly rooting and the thrusting necessity to seek for plenitude elsewhere, is containable. But for certain French Romantics at the beginning of the nineteenth century the uneasy interface of reality and spirituality deepens into existential crisis. Chateaubriand (1768–1848) is the first to define what he calls "the rootless indeterminacy of the passions" ("le vague des passions"), seeing in it both the "evil" and the "malady" with which society of his time is stricken (the ambiguity in "le mal de siècle" is probably deliberate). "We are disillusioned without ever having taken pleasure in existence," he writes; "we still have desires, but no illusions. Imagination is rich, abundant, a source of wonder; but existence is impoverished, desiccated and disenchanting. We live with a full heart in an empty world, and without ever having made full use of anything are disabused of all."[14] So too with Senancour (1770–1846), who in his epistolary novel *Obermann* (1804) gives intense expression to an all-pervading sense of disquiet and inner turmoil: "There is within me an uneasiness which will never be still [...]. There is an infinite distance between what I am and what I need to be. Love is immense, it is not boundless. [...] I want to hope, I should wish to know! I need limitless illusions, ever receding so as constantly to deceive me" (Letter 18).[15]

In the context of this exacerbated tension, an integral part of the anguish generated is felt by others to devolve directly from the inadequacy of language itself. Part of the problem lies in the feeling that the divine, in which the Word is magisterially enshrined, does not communicate with man. Musset's Rolla rejects holy Writ ("I do not believe, oh Christ! in your holy word:/I have come too late into a world too old");[16] the questions asked by Vigny's Christ in Gethsemane remain unanswered, and in the face of this silence the poet's only possible recourse is to a parallel disdain, juxtaposing a "cold silence" with the eternal one of the divine.[17] Nor is religious anguish the only context where the corrosive effects of linguistic uneasiness may be perceived. The latter extend inexorably to man's response to nature: for many Romantic writers a source of inspiration, integration and self-identification, nature in its abundance can also step outside the conventional registers of articulation, posing challenges which even Chateaubriand—that master of finely wrought French prose—has difficulty in meeting. The challenge associated with rendering the pristine strangeness of the New World in particular: to be lost for words is to be worlds away, the equation between the two being forcefully stated when Chateaubriand contemplates the Niagara Falls for the first time ("The grandeur, the astonishing melancholy of this spectacle could not be expressed in human tongue; the most magnificent nights that Europe has to offer cannot give an idea of it").[18]

The negative connotations experienced in expression are of course not unilateral. It is interesting to compare Chateaubriand's view with that of one of his German contemporaries, Wilhelm Wackenroder (1773–98), who, despite death at only twenty-five, wrote an influential essay in 1797 entitled "On Two Wondrous Languages and Their Mysterious Power". If by language, that "precious gift from Heaven", we have managed to "establish our ascendancy over the entire world", the divine presence still escapes it ("Only the invisible stands beyond translation into our soul by words. [...] When we hear speak of God's sovereign goodness [...], useless sounds fill our ears without elevating our soul, as language ought to do").[19] But Wackenroder sees other, figurative, languages capable of taking its place, those of nature herself and of art. The empathy created between living beings and living things distils its own secret idiom, an idea which, via the Swedish mystic Swedenborg, will later in the nineteenth century prove of crucial significance in the elaboration of Baudelaire's view of the "correspondences" which give meaning to man's place in the world, or in Nerval's embracing synthesis of human destiny, encapsulated only by the power of poetry, by that "Golden Verse" which concludes his celebrated collection of sonnets, *The Chimaerae* (1854).[20]

For Novalis, the secret of interpreting the "infinite" and "inexhaustible variability" of nature lies rather in what he terms the necessity to "exaggerate" poetic diction (*The Disciples in Saïs* [1795], II, "Nature"). Poets, by virtue of their very "improper", figurative use of language, are exceptionally suited to apprehending "forces within their control, worlds obedient to them". In a free-flowing interplay from which the anguish associated with inadequate linguistic means seems to be banished, nature is said to "express" the inner and outer states of man, in all his self-appointed superiority and strangeness.[21] To a degree, this explains how, in his novel *Heinrich von Ofterdingen* (1801) and the celebrated quest for the "blue flower", Novalis can speak as freely and confidently as he does of the "infinite", the "unknown", the "incomprehensible", the "indescribable", the "irresistible" and the "unspeakable" (Part I, Chapter 1), in a concatenated series of superlative absolutes which realize the shifting subtleties of a vision in metamorphosis, where the risks of approximation or capitulation are not felt.[22]

But these signal victories over the difficulties of expression are not unqualified in literary representations of the Romantic spirit. With an intense psychological and emotional resonance, Emily Brontë's *Wuthering Heights* (1847) locates in the hallowed Romantic ideal of Goethe's "elective affinity" a deeply transgressive message, that of an instinctive identification between Catherine and Heathcliff, impervious to the moralizing and normalizing conventions of accepted social conduct. It is in the very depth of the passionate fusion which possesses the two characters—an ambivalent and highly complex intermingling of cruelty and compulsion, of the human and the inhuman—that the obligation to express is placed in delicate and disturbing counterpoint with language's potential to do so. This is not to say that particular effects of style need consciously to be sought for their sophistication or their overt transgression of the stuff of everyday expression. Brontë's style is generally remarkable for the directness and simplicity of its texture, for the elemental bluntness of its engagement with natural forces, where the extraordinary nature of the bond between Catherine and Heathcliff is paradoxically explored in terms of the matter-of-fact. But even the subtlety of this middle course, where the overriding and impassioned recognition of the other as self is articulated in a seething primary substratum of repressed and sometimes overt violence, the articulate continuity of expression can at times fragment. Catherine, in conversation with Nelly Dean, cannot define the nature of the feeling she experiences, but only communicate it in terms of projected consequence, comparison or accentuated affirmation:

> Every Linton on the face of the earth might melt into nothing, before I could consent to forsake Heathcliff! Oh that's not what I intend—that's not what I mean! [...] If all else perished and *he* remained, I should still continue to be; and if all else remained, and he were annihilated, the universe would turn to a mighty stranger. [...] My love for Heathcliff is like the foliage in the woods [resembling] the eternal rocks beneath [...]. Nelly, I *am* Heathcliff.[23]

The difficulties created when self and other, reality and the supernatural, are experienced in their radical conjunction, are confirmed by Gérard de Nerval's novel *Aurélia* (1855): "I do not know how to explain that, in my mind, earthly events could coincide with supernatural ones: that is easier to *feel* than to articulate with clarity. What then was this spirit which was both myself and beyond me?"[24]

Writing on religion in 1830, the year of the Romantic triumph in France epitomized by the performance of Hugo's historical play *Hernani* in that bastion of classical conservatism, the Comédie Française, Benjamin Constant summarizes what is felt by many to be, in language, not a part of God's gift to man but a source of inadequacy and distortion:

> All our inmost feelings seem to elude the grasp of language. The rebellious word, by the very fact of generalizing what it expresses, serves to designate and to distinguish, rather than to define. As an instrument of the mind it is only good at conveying the notions of the mind. It fails in anything which has to do with the senses, on the one hand, or the soul, on the other.[25]

The value of this comment is that it both circumscribes some of the deepest, defining tensions which give Romantic sensibility the vibrancy of its dynamic exploration of all that is beyond man's immediate situation, and also marks the demise of the very confidence in the self's central status as physical and metaphysical point of reference, a primordial tenet in the Romantic canon. In 1856, at a time when artistic and literary perception had already turned emphatically away from the kind of Byronic and Hugolian exaltation which marked the high point of Romanticism in Europe, Flaubert's *Madame Bovary* gave voice to the full consequences of demands placed on language which it had difficulty in meeting. The exaggerated sentimental clichés and conventional protestations of affection which Emma Bovary uncritically assimilates from her Romantic reading are by then a degenerate form of articulateness, swept aside with cynical manipulation by her sated lover, Rodolphe. But Flaubert, with supreme irony, in one of the most lyrically articulate passages of his novels, attempts to rehabilitate not just the values of sincerity and authenticity in his heroine, but also, through his richly textured prose, the worth of language itself:

> So full of experience though Rodolphe was, he could not distinguish the difference in the emotions beneath the similarity of the expression [...]: as if the fulness of the soul did not sometimes brim over in the emptiest of metaphors, since no one, ever, can give the exact measure of his needs, his ideas or his sorrows, for human speech is like a cracked cauldron on which we beat our tunes good for bears to dance to when we are trying to touch the heart of the stars.[26]

It is from these roots in Romanticism that what was held to be the corrupting power of language turned increasingly, in the second half of the nineteenth century and beyond, towards interiorization and self-reference. Self-reference was no longer understood in terms of the Romantic imposition of self on world and the Promethean promotion of the individual, but far more as the problematical source of unstable, relativized angles of vision, touching both upon the specifics of perception and the attitude of the narrating voice towards the creation of its own text. Whether or not we agree with them, subsequent twentieth-century developments in French thought may in part be traced to the problematical role which Romanticism, through the action of its conceptual components themselves, conferred on language. That influence may be perceived perhaps most clearly along subsequent phenomenological and structural lines, whereby the self is held to structure the world according to its own limited and relative codes of coherence, thereby rendering the nature of both self and world deeply problematical. The link back to the stresses and strains of the Romantic ethos may also be seen in certain modern extensions of the interfacing between psychoanalysis and literature, most notably in Lacan's grounding conception of language as lack, unco-ordinated and defective in the subject's acquisition and use of it, in the interstices of which the self and its complexes are highlighted. So too, in other European literature, particularly Italian, the impact of self-referentiality as a ramification of the ambitious aspirations of Romanticism is clearly evident. The work of Luigi Pirandello, Italo Calvino and Umberto Eco in exploring respectively the richness of the self-reflexive work and of the open-ended one, standing radically apart from notions of teleological ordering or authorial omnipotence, restates with modern variations what certain eminent Romantic writers saw as language's power of deformation, compounded through its lack of precise, defining authority by an increasing mistrust of definitive foreclosure.

For increasingly, character portrayal stumbles on the inexplicable depths of psychological motivation which, even when psychology has ostensibly been investigated, remain largely indeterminate and unclarified. The rise and fall of Stendhal's Julien Sorel in *Le Rouge et le Noir* is a study in the growing autonomy of the protagonist, resolutely unheeding of the narrator's injunctions and wishes, with major consequences for the very conception of the novel and its functioning. And towards the end of the nineteenth century, in Dostoevsky and Gide, the arbitrary, irrational impulses of unmotivated acts will be given pride of place, as writers take full measure of the mysteries of feelings and emotions, as too of their potential in restructuring and reorganizing the principles governing the novel's form.

I wish finally to place emphasis on one aspect of the whole problematic of language's functioning, where being "lost for words" takes on a peculiarly generative resonance. In treating those moments when language appears no longer to be able to cope with the complexity of European Romanticism's conceptual or experiential aspirations, I have necessarily had to confront the subject in a largely negative way. Instances where language is felt to be inadequate could scarcely be interpreted otherwise: Emma Bovary's wholesale assimilation of worn-out Romantic clichés is attributable to an inherent inability to express the self, a dilemma whose properly tragic dimension should not be neglected. But at the same time, there exists the possibility of a creative overlapping between language and silence, as George Steiner has eloquently demonstrated. In his *Tractatus Logico-philosophicus* Wittgenstein circumscribes perfectly the tension between the limitation of the subject's experience or knowledge of the world through language, and the possibility of the existence of things, despite the impossibility of speaking logically about them: "The world is *my* world: this is manifest in the fact that the limits of *language* (of that language which I alone understand) mean the limits of *my* world." Yet limitation here does not constitute foreclosure, as the concluding propositions make clear ("There are, indeed, things that cannot be put into words. They *make themselves manifest*. They are what is mystical"). The counterbalancing of limitation with the paradoxical potentiality of the inexpressible leads to Wittgenstein's celebrated final comment, where silence is postulated, in the light of the "manifestation" of inexpressible things, as peculiarly pregnant with untold virtuality ("What we cannot speak about we must pass over in silence").[27]

In the light of these remarks, the validity which we might otherwise see in André Breton's famous quip concerning "meaning" in the poetry of his fellow Surrealist Saint-Pol Roux ("If Saint-Pol Roux had meant to write that, he would have written it") may seem strangely reductive.[28] A study could well be devoted to the status of blanks, interruptions, unfinished processes of conclusion or instances of suspension in the manuscripts of the Romantics, where such manuscripts exist. It may well be, as Wittengenstein suggests, that the complexities in the distribution of writing on the page, and the interplay of failing language with the expressive potential of the space surrounding it, confer on moments of loss in articulate communication a strangely evocative, "manifestative" power, which the subsequent typographical normalization wrought by publication has itself unjustly distorted and misinterpreted.

## NOTES

1   Charles Dickens, *The Life and Adventures of Nicholas Nickleby* (London, Educational Book Company, 1910), p. 295.

2   Alessandro Manzoni, *I promessi sposi*, edited by G. Testori (Milan, Mondadori, 1984), p. 346: "Chi potrà ora descrivere il terrore, l'angoscia di costei, esprimere ciò che passava nel suo animo?"

3   Alessandro Manzoni, *I promessi sposi*, p. 342: "Quel Dio di cui aveva sentito parlare, ma che, da gran tempo, non si curava di negare né di riconoscere, occupato soltanto a vivere come se non ci fosse, ora, in certi momenti d'abbattimento senza motivo, di terrore senza pericolo, gli

pareva sentirlo gridar dentro di sé: Io sono però. Nel primo bollor delle passioni, la legge che aveva, se non altro, sentita annunziare in nome di Lui, non gli era parsa che odiosa: ora, quando gli tornava d'improvviso alla mente, la mente, suo malgrado, la concepiva come una cosa che ha il suo adempimento."

4    Alessandro Manzoni, *I promessi sposi*, p. 336.

5    "Et sur l'Académie, aïeule et douairière,/Cachant sous ses jupons les tropes effarés,/Et sur les bataillons d'alexandrins carrés,/Je fis souffler un vent révolutionnaire,/Je mis un bonnet rouge au vieux dictionnaire": Victor Hugo, "Réponse à un acte d'accusation", in his *Les Contemplations*, edited by P. Albouy (Paris, Gallimard, 1973), p. 43.

6    Paul Valéry, *Œuvres*, edited by J. Hytier, 2 vols (Paris, Gallimard, 1957), I, 604.

7    Samuel Taylor Coleridge, *Biographia Literaria* (Princeton, Princeton University Press; London, Routledge and Kegan Paul, 1983) [= *The Collected Works of Samuel Taylor Coleridge*, VII], Part I, Ch. 9, p. 148.

8    Charles Baudelaire, "Salon of 1846", in *Curiosités esthétiques: l'art romantique*, edited by H. Lemaitre (Paris, Garnier, 1962), p. 103.

9    Samuel Taylor Coleridge, *Biographia Literaria*, Part II, Ch. 14, p. 5.

10   Samuel Taylor Coleridge, "The Rime of the Ancyent Marinere" in his *Poems* (London, Campbell, 1991).

11   Among many examples, two of the most vivid are: "Yea, slimy things did crawl with legs/Upon the slimy sea" and "The water, like a witch's oils,/Burnt green and blue and white" (Part II).

12   Ludwig Uhland, "On Romanticism", quoted in *Le Romantisme européen*, edited by A. Biedermann (Paris, Larousse, 1972), vol. I, p. 102.

13   Novalis, *Fragments*, 1801, quoted in *Le Romantisme européen*, I, 111: "Poetry is the representation of the soul, of the inner world in its totality. Words, its intermediaries, signal this from the start, for they are the external manifestation of this profound realm. Poetic awareness has many points in common with a mystical one. It is the awareness of all that is particularized, personal, unknown, mysterious, of all that must be revealed, of everything which is both chance and necessity. It expresses the inexpressible. It sees the invisible; it touches the intangible. Poetry is reality in its absolute state. That is the central reference of my philosophy. The more a thing is poetic, the more it is true."

14   F-R. de Chateaubriand, *Le Génie du christianisme* [1802], edited by M. Regard (Paris, Gallimard, 1978), III. 2. 9.

15   E. P. de Senancour, *Obermann*, edited by G. Michaut (Paris, Droz, 1931), p. 74.

16   Alfred de Musset, *Rolla* [1833], in his *Œuvres complètes*, edited by P. V. Tieghem (Paris, Seuil, 1963), p. 139.

17   Alfred de Vigny, "Le Mont des Oliviers", in *Les Destinées* [1844]. See *Poèmes antiques et modernes: Les Destinées*, edited by A. Jarry (Paris, Gallimard, 1973), p. 195.

18   F-R. de Chateaubriand, *Le Génie du christianisme*, I. 5. 12: "La gran-

deur, l'étonnante mélancolie de ce tableau ne saurait s'exprimer dans les langues humaines; les plus belles nuits en Europe ne peuvent en donner une idée" (p. 592).

19  Wilhelm Wackenroder, "Von zwei wunderbaren Sprachen und deren geheimnisvoller Kraft", quoted in *Le Romantisme européen*, I, 201 (my translation).

20  Gérard de Nerval, *Œuvres*, edited by J. Richer (Paris, Gallimard, 1952), pp. 34–35.

21  Novalis, *Die Lehrlinge von Sais*, quoted in *Le Romantisme européen*, I, 193.

22  Novalis, *Heinrich von Ofterdingen*, quoted in *Le Romantisme européen*, II, 58, 60.

23  Emily Brontë, *Wuthering Heights* (Harmondsworth, Penguin, 1965), pp. 121–22.

24  Gérard de Nerval, *Aurélia (Les Filles du feu)*, in his *Œuvres*, pp. 380–81.

25  Benjamin Constant, *Œuvres*, edited by A. Roulin (Paris, Gallimard, 1957), pp. 1381–82 ("De la religion considérée dans sa source, ses formes et ses développements"): "Tous nos sentiments intimes semblent se jouer des efforts du langage: la parole rebelle, par cela seul qu'elle généralise ce qu'elle exprime, sert à désigner, à distinguer, plutôt qu'à définir. Instrument de l'esprit, elle ne rend bien que les notions de l'esprit. Elle échoue dans tout ce qui tient, d'une part aux sens et de l'autre l'âme."

26  Gustave Flaubert, *Œuvres*, edited by A. Thibaudet and R. Dumesnil (Paris, Gallimard, 1951), vol. I, p. 466 (Part II, Ch. 12): "Il ne distinguait pas, cet homme si plein de pratique, la dessemblance des sentiments sous la parité des expressions. [...] comme si la plénitude de l'âme ne débordait pas quelquefois par les métaphores les plus vides, puisque personne, jamais, ne peut donner l'exacte mesure de ses besoins, ni de ses conceptions, ni de ses douleurs, et que la parole humaine est comme un chaudron fêlé où nous battons des mélodies à faire danser les ours, quand on voudrait attendrir les étoiles."

27  Ludwig Wittgenstein, *Tractatus Logico-philosophicus*, translated by D. F. Pears and B. F. McGuinness (London, Routledge and Kegan Paul, 1961), v. 62 (p. 115), vi. 522 (p. 151), vii (p. 151).

28  Quoted in J-P. Sartre, *Qu'est-ce que la littérature?* (Paris, Gallimard, 1948), p. 24: "S'il avait voulu le dire, il l'aurait dit."

# LORCA'S *BODAS DE SANGRE* AND SYNGE'S *RIDERS TO THE SEA*

## Stephen F. Boyd

Although *Bodas de sangre* and *Riders to the Sea* were written some thirty years apart, in different languages and reflecting different cultural backgrounds, it may be argued that there is considerable affinity of spirit between them. My objective is to elucidate this affinity and also to point out some significant differences between the two plays—differences which, apart from the obvious disparity in scale, seem to me to be largely matters of focus and nuance.

The affinity is not merely one of coincidence, for, as is well known, one of Lorca's friends in Granada, Miguel Cerón, read *Riders to the Sea* to him in 1922, translating spontaneously from English to Spanish.[1] A translation by the poet Juan Ramón Jiménez and his wife, Zenobia Camprubí, had been published two years earlier, but it is not certain that Lorca ever read it.[2] According to Cerón himself, Lorca's reaction to the Irish play was one of enormous enthusiasm.[3] Almost undoubtedly, in Synge's Aran Islands setting, with its isolation, its living folk traditions, its fatalistic Catholicism, its people living close to and aware of elemental and telluric forces, and in their graphic, almost poetic speech, Lorca would have seen an analogue of his native Andalucía. The atmosphere of fatality would also have made a strong appeal to him, for both artistic and personal reasons.[4]

The impact of *Riders to the Sea* remained latent for some ten years, for it was not until 1932 that Lorca wrote *Bodas de sangre*, and by that time the influence of Synge had combined with that of a newspaper article which appeared in *ABC* on 25 July 1928. This reported an extraordinary crime which had taken place three days earlier in the small village of Níjar in the province of Almería. On the day of her wedding a bride had abandoned her husband-to-be and eloped with her childhood sweetheart. The lover had been shot dead in an ambush and the bride left half-strangled by her own sister, who wanted to vindicate the family honour. This event captured Lorca's imagination—so much so that he used it as the basis for the plot of *Bodas de sangre*. In the play the bride elopes on her wedding-day with her former lover, Leonardo, who is now a married man. She earlier refused, or was not allowed, to marry him, because he was too poor. The bridegroom goes in pursuit of the eloping couple, and he and Leonardo stab each other to death during a fight on a river bank. This struggle takes place off stage, and all the audience hears is the loud cries of the dying men. Importantly, Leonardo and the bridegroom belong to rival, feuding families, and Leonardo's family has previously been responsible for the deaths of the bridegroom's father and elder brother.

The way in which history repeats itself, coming full circle, and the feeling created from the beginning that this is fated to happen, are important features that the two plays have in common. In each play it is the central female figure (the bridegroom's mother and Maurya) who has a strong presentiment of death. Maurya has lost six sons, a husband and a father-in-law to the power of the sea; the mother in *Bodas de sangre* has lost her husband and eldest son in a blood vendetta with another family. Each woman has only one son left and each feels that he will be killed in the same way as his father and brother(s). As *Bodas de sangre* opens, the Bridegroom is going out to work in the vineyard. His mother, in protective mood, is afraid that he may not return:

> And then he just doesn't come back. Or if he does, it's only so that you can lay out his body, and rub it with salt so that it doesn't bloat in the heat.[5]

Similarly, in *Riders to the Sea* Maurya is anxious to prevent Bartley sailing to Galway to sell horses at the fair:

> It's hard set we'll be surely the day you're drowned with the rest. What way will I live and the girls with me, and I an old woman looking for the grave?[6]

In Synge's play the circle of recurrence is much more tightly drawn because the body of Bartley's brother Michael has just been found washed up on the Donegal coast and some of his clothes have been sent to the family for identification. That identification is only positively made just before Bartley's body, wrapped in a sail, is brought into the house. Here, past and present overlap and coalesce. In *Bodas de sangre* the time-lapse between one death and another is much greater but the sense of inevitability is no less strong because the violent ends of the Mother's husband and eldest son are still very much present in her memory and imagination. To reinforce this sense of cyclical tragedy mention is made, towards the end of the first scene, of a young neighbour, Rafael, who just the other day had his "arm sliced clean off" by a harvesting machine (p. 35).[7]

Both writers also use reference to weather conditions to underline the atmosphere of fatality. In Synge the strong wind blows the door of the house open, and there are frequent mentions of its power to stir up the sea. In Lorca an atmosphere of oppressive heat is evoked:

MOTHER   The sun's scorching hot.
NEIGHBOUR   The lads running water to the reapers are fed up with
  it. (p. 37)[8]

And later:

BRIDE   It's so hot inside.
MAID   In these parts there's not even a breath of cool air at dawn.
  (p. 55)[9]

Naturally, since *Bodas de sangre* is a full-length play, the sense of foreboding is created in a more sustained way and by a greater variety of means. For example, the Mother-in-law's lullaby in Act I Scene 2 looks forward in a subtle and unobtrusive manner, through its imagery of horses, water and blood, to what will happen later:

The horse is weeping,
his wounded hooves
and poor, poor
frozen mane
and in his eye
a silver dagger shone.
Down to the river,
down to the stream,
all the way down
blood flows fuller
than water. (pp. 39–40)[10]

In fact it is a feature of Lorca's play that poetic imagery is realized in dramatic action. In a somewhat less subtle way this also happens in *Riders to the Sea*, most notably when Maurya describes how Patch's drowned body was brought home:

> MAURYA I looked out then, and there were men coming after them, and they holding a thing in the half of a red sail and water dripping out of it—it was a dry day, Nora—and leaving a track to the door. (pp. 27–28)

Almost immediately afterwards Nora sees the men approaching the house with Bartley's body:

> NORA They're carrying a thing among them, and there's water dripping out of it and leaving a track by the big stones. [...] (*[...]* Then men carry in the body of* BARTLEY, *laid on a plank, with a bit of sail over it, and lay it on the table.*) (p. 38)

Apart from the fact that fate is virtually an unseen protagonist in both plays, the other major feature they have in common is their use of the supernatural. In *Riders to the Sea* Maurya gives Bartley, who is already on his way down to the sea, a piece of bread, and has a very disturbing vision:

> MAURYA I'm after seeing him this day, and he riding and galloping. Bartley came first on the red mare, and I tried to say "God speed you", but something choked the words in my throat. He went by quickly; and "The blessing of God on you," says he, and I crying, at the grey pony, and there was Michael upon it—with fine clothes on him, and new shoes on his feet. (pp. 26–27)

Having seen this, she is certain that Bartley is going to die, and in fact after Bartley's body is brought in we hear that the grey pony knocked him into the sea. According to Ramón Sainero ghostly riders emerging from the sea or a lake are quite common in Irish folklore;[11] their appearance always heralds a new death. Therefore this supernatural episode in the play is probably not based on Synge's imagination alone. The ghostly rider would appear to be an incarnation of the power of the sea itself and, according to Sainero again, the Aran Islanders have a strong superstitious respect for the sea—so much so that they will not rescue a drowning man because they feel that he belongs to it.

In *Bodas de sangre*, unlike *Riders to the Sea*, the supernatural actually appears on stage in the form of the Moon, dressed as a young woodcutter with whitened face, and of an old Beggar Woman who is covered from head to toe in a mantle of dark green rags. Both appear to represent death, and certainly the moon as a symbol of death is abundantly present throughout Lorca's work. Although the association of the moon and death is ancient, it is very much a personal symbol for Lorca and he always treats it in a personal and individual fashion. There is, however, one folkloric element in its use in *Bodas de sangre*, arising from the fact that in certain parts of southern Spain "The Man in the Moon" was thought to be a young woodcutter.[12] The representation of death as a beggar woman, on the other hand, may not owe anything to the European folk tradition, but is certainly reminiscent of the old, withered man who confronts the "ritoures thre" in Chaucer's *Pardoner's Tale*. He too is completely covered in a cloak and wanders the earth looking for final rest.[13]

In Synge's play the whole community, particularly Maurya, is aware of the sea as something more than just a natural phenomenon. We are presented with what could be called a community vision. In Lorca the characters are aware of the moonlight and the Bridegroom actually meets and talks to the Beggar Woman, but no one is aware of the presence of anything supernatural. The deaths of the two young men are explicable in purely natural, rational terms: they kill each other in a fight. The presence of the Moon and the Beggar Woman, however, offers the audience another perspective, that of an ultimately malign and cruel force lying below the surface of everyday reality. Instead of a community vision, as in Synge, we have a personal one which corresponds closely to what we find elsewhere in Lorca's work, both literary and other (in his letters, for example). Lorca's focus could also, perhaps, be seen as more "universal" since the supernatural power in his play is death itself. My feeling that Lorca's vision of the supernatural is more personal is also due, in large measure, to the fact that the Moon and the Beggar Woman speak in verse which is full the quasi-surrealist imagery that one finds elsewhere in Lorca. The voice is unmistakably his:

> MOON  The moon leaves a knife hanging in the sky,
> a cold trap of lead
> that seeks blood's warm cry.
> Let me in! I come frozen and numbed
> through walls and glass!
> Open your homes and breasts

so that I can warm myself.
I'm freezing. (*Blood Wedding*, p. 85)[14]

Because of the presence of the Moon and the Beggar Woman on stage, and because of the poetic language they use, the supernatural is much more intense and electric in Lorca than in Synge, where it is comparatively gentle and blurred. Death in the Spanish play, in both imagery and action, is also much more violent and passionate than in *Riders to the Sea*. It involves personal enmity and bloodshed, the penetration of the flesh by a knife. In fact, these remarks could be applied to a contrast between the whole, overall effects of the two plays. *Bodas de sangre* is pitched higher (not in a qualitative sense) and its emotions are more acute. This is not just a question of the language (though it is also that, particularly the prevalent use of verse in Act III), but also of the settings, which are not realist as they are in *Riders to the Sea*. Instead they are highly stylized and, especially in the last scene, quite "unrealistic". For example, Lorca specifies the setting for Act II Scene 2 as follows:

> Outside the BRIDE's home. Tones of greyish white and cold blue. The whole atmosphere is sombre and silvery. Large cacti. In the background brownish hills in sharp relief, as though painted on ceramics. (p. 69)[15]

These differences, of course, reflect not merely the personal sensibilities of the two writers, but the difference in time and generation. Lorca's play is, at least partially, experimental and shows the influence of the surrealist movement, though it is not strictly a surrealist play. One might sum up these differences in mode and effect (if a little fancifully) by using images which are central to the two plays: the difference between the sullen, diffuse light of the sea (Synge) and the glitter of a knife (Lorca).

In both plays the tragic victims are not just individuals but principally whole communities (mostly the women of these communities), and in both there is a strong element of ritual grief and poetic lament. Here again there is a great affinity of spirit and, at one point, of language, involving a striking motif which represents the closest Lorca comes to a direct, material debt to Synge. Here are the laments of the two mothers over their dead sons:

> MAURYA They're all gone, and there isn't anything more the sea can do to me... I'll have no call now to be up crying and praying when

the wind breaks from the south, and you can hear the surf is in the east and the surf is in the west, making a great stir with the two noises, and they hitting one on the other. I'll have no call now to be going down and getting Holy Water in the dark nights after Samhain, and I won't care what way the sea is when the other women will be keening... but it's a great rest I'll have... It's a great rest I'll have now, and great sleeping in the nights after Samhain... (*Riders to the Sea*, p. 29)

MOTHER  I want to be here. In peace and quiet. They're all dead now. But I'll sleep easy tonight, free from the fear of guns and knives. Tonight it'll be other women who lean out into the rain watching for their sons. But not me. I'll sleep... and my sleep will be like a cold marble dove carrying the white flowers and frost to his grave... consecrated ground... consecrated! No. It's not consecrated; it's a bed of clay to hold them in the sky. (*Blood Wedding*, p. 100)[16]

In both plays elements of Catholic ritual are present. Maurya sprinkles Bartley's body with holy water and the women in *Bodas de sangre* chant a hymn to the cross:

> Sweet nails,
> Sweet cross,
> Sweet name
> Of Jesus. (p. 104)[17]

But despite the invocation of the Christian God in both plays, He is felt to be remote, inscrutable, even impotent; and in both cases an atmosphere of empty, fatalistic desolation pervades the ending:

MOTHER  What does anything at all matter to me? Blessed be the wheat, because my sons lie beneath it; blessed be the rain, because it wets the faces of the dead. Blessed be God, who lays us all down together to rest.[18]

Although both mothers are resigned to the loss of their last remaining sons, the Mother of *Bodas de sangre* expresses her grief more passionately and her desolation is mingled with bitterness. The last words of *Riders to the Sea* are words of helpless resignation:

MAURYA  Bartley will have a fine coffin out of the white boards, and a deep grave surely. What more can we want than that? No man at all can be living for ever, and we must be satisfied. (p. 30)

*Bodas de sangre* ends on a more violent note, and the Mother's final words express a kind of muted outrage at the fact that by the shedding of blood a human life can be brought to an end:

> It [a knife] fits so snug in
> the hand, but slices so quick
> through the startled flesh
> and there it stops, at the point
> where trembling enmeshed,
> lies the dark root of the scream. (p. 105)[19]

There is a strong element of beauty in the laments of the two plays but the language of Lorca's characters is one of more exalted and even, at times, luxuriant lyricism.

Some of the divergences of the plays have been examined, principally those due to differences in artistic temperament, generation and culture; but obviously the major difference remains one of scale. There is a greater variety of mood in Lorca, facilitated by the greater length of his play. There is even a moment of comedy. *Bodas de sangre* is also thematically richer and preoccupied not only with fate but with the interplay of fate and free will, sexual passion and the distinctive Hispanic code of sexual honour. It would be interesting to compare the status of these two plays as tragedies, especially given the influence of classical Greek tragedy on Lorca; but that is a subject for another study.

As to the extent of Lorca's debt to Synge, it is obvious that there is an influence, but an influence that has been totally absorbed into the subconscious, totally internalized. Lorca, when he heard *Riders to the Sea* read to him, would probably have had a sense of recognition rather than revelation. It would have been an encounter with an ethos that was already partially familiar to him because of his background in rural Andalucía and because of his intensely personal preoccupation with fate and death. In the words of Lorca's most recent and most distinguished biographer, Ian Gibson:

> Perhaps, bearing in mind the work of the Irishman, Lorca realized that to write a tragedy in the twentieth century it was not necessary to indulge in the useless exercise of recreating those of ancient Greece—which he did however read assiduously—but rather he could look for inspiration in a community, in this case that of Andalucía, which still had not lost its roots and the telluric sense of life.[20]

## NOTES

1  For an account of this see I. Gibson, *Federico García Lorca*, vol. II
   (Barcelona, Grijalbo, 1987), p. 208.

2  J. M. Synge, *Jinetes hacia el mar*, translated by J. R. Jiménez and Z.
   Camprubí de Jiménez (Madrid, Editores, 1920).

3  I. Gibson, *Federico García Lorca*, p. 208.

4  For a similar view, see the prologue by Esteban Pujals to Ramón Sainero
   Sánchez's book, *Lorca y Synge: ¿un mundo maldito?* (Madrid, Editorial
   de la Universidad Complutense, 1983), pp. 11–12.

5  F. García Lorca, *Blood Wedding*, translated by D. Johnston (London
   etc., Hodder and Stoughton, 1989), p. 31. All subsequent quotations
   in English from the play, except one (see n. 18), are taken from this
   translation, and page references follow them in the text. Footnotes
   attached to such quotations refer to the original Spanish version, *Bodas
   de sangre* (Madrid, Espasa Calpe, Colección Austral, 1987). The
   original Spanish version of this quotation is: "Y ese hombre no vuelve.
   O si vuelve es para ponerle una palma encima o un plato de sal gorda
   para que no se hinche" (p. 47).

6  J. M. Synge, *Plays, Poems and Prose* (London, Everyman, 1972), p. 22.
   All subsequent references to *Riders to the Sea* are based on this edition.
   Hereafter page references appear in the main text.

7  "VECINA Hace dos días trajeron al hijo de mi vecina con los dos brazos
   cortados por la máquina" (*Bodas de sangre*, p. 55).

8  "MADRE ¿Has visto qué día de calor?/VECINA Iban negros los chiquillos
   que llevan el agua a los segadores" (*Bodas de sangre*, p. 60).

9  "NOVIA No se puede estar ahí dentro, del calor./CRIADA En estas tierras
   no refresca ni al amancer" (*Bodas de sangre*, p. 89).

10 "Que el caballo se pone a llorar./Las patas heridas,/las crines heladas,/
   dentro de los ojos/un puñal de plata./Bajaban al río./¡Ay, cómo bajaban!/
   La sangre corría/más fuerte que el agua" (*Bodas de sangre*, p. 62).

11 "Horsemen from beyond the grave, emerging from lake or sea are, as
   witnessed by a whole series of legends, figures of ill omen since their
   appearance heralds a new death. The horse and figure of a dead man
   previously drowned in the water may possibly be connected with the
   superstitious fear of the waters as a magical destroyer of human life.
   These ghostly horsemen were known to the classical world, and in the
   Iberian peninsula also, there are many accounts of supernatural horses":
   R. Sainero, *Leyendas celtas* (Madrid, Akal, 1985), pp. 152–53 (translation mine). Sainero does not document this tradition.

12 See C. B. Morris, *García Lorca, "Bodas de sangre": A Critical Guide*
   (London, Grant and Cutler, 1980), p. 19. Morris refers to the popular
   Spanish legend but does not disclose his source.

13   "And on the ground, which is my moodres gate,/I knokke with with my staff, both erly and late/And seye 'Leeve mooder, leet me in!/Lo how I vanysshe, flesh, and blood, and skyn!/Allas! whan shul my bones been at reste?'": *The Works of Geoffrey Chaucer*, edited by F. N. Robinson (London, Oxford University Press, 1970), p. 152 (ll. 729–33).

14   "LUNA   La luna deja un cuchillo/abandonado en el aire,/que siendo acecho de plomo/quiere ser dolor de sangre./¡Dejamde entrar! ¡Vengo helada/por paredes y cristales!/¡Abrid tejados y pechos/donde pueda calentarme!/¡Tengo frío!" (*Bodas de sangre*, p. 144).

15   "Exterior de la cueva de la NOVIA. Entonación en blancos grises y azules fríos. Grandes chumberas. Tonos sombríos y plateados. Panorama de mesetas color barquillo, todo endurecido como paisaje de céramica popular" (*Bodas de sangre*, p. 144).

16   "MADRE   Aquí. Aquí quiero estar. Y tranquila. Ya todos están muertos. A medianoche dormiré sin que ya me aterren la escopeta o el cuchillo. Otras madres se asomarán a las ventanas, azotadas por la lluvia, para ver el rostro de sus hijos. Yo, no. Yo haré con mi sueño una fría paloma de marfil que llevecamelias de escarcha sobre el camposanto, no, camposanto, no; lecho de tierra, cama que los cobija y que los mece por el cielo" (*Bodas de sangre*, p. 166).

17   "Dulces clavos/dulce cruz,/dulce nombre/de Jesús" (*Bodas de sangre*, p. 171).

18   Translation mine. The original version is: "MADRE   ¿Qué me importa a mí nada de nada? Benditos sean los trigos, porque mis hijos están debajo de ellos, bendita sea la lluvia, porque moja la cara de los muertos. Bendito sea Dios, que nos tiende juntos para descansar."

19   "Y apenas cabe en la mano,/pero que penetra frío/por las carnes asombradas/y allí se para, en el sitio/donde tiembla enmarañada/la oscura raíz del grito" (*Bodas de sangre*, p. 172).

20   I. Gibson, *Federico García Lorca*, p. 208 (translation mine).

# FRUITFUL DISSONANCE: THE LIFE AND WORK OF REINHOLD SCHNEIDER

## J. Henry O'Shea

It is not unusual for a writer who has been well-known and influential while living to be quickly forgotten, together with his writings, after he has died. Reinhold Schneider was unknown in the English-speaking world during his lifetime and, since his death in 1958, has been virtually forgotten in the German-speaking world. The purpose of this essay is to give a brief outline of Schneider's life and the recurring themes of his writings, making reference to his autobiographical works, *Verhüllter Tag* (1954) and *Winter in Wien* (1958).

Although in his earlier years Schneider denied the importance of a writer's biographical data, in later life he came to admit that these, particularly the surroundings and experiences of his earliest years, had a determining role. Schneider was born in Baden-Baden in 1903. His Catholic mother and Protestant father owned a successful and fashionable hotel, frequented by the highest of European society, among them, in an earlier period, the German imperial family. Although he was raised as a Catholic, Schneider's religion was conventional and superficial, a consequence of the confessional truce between his parents, which had marginalized questions of commitment. While distant from both parents as a result of their business preoccupations, Schneider was closer to his father. From him he later claimed to have inherited the melancholy that was to mark his life and writings. In addition, Schneider brought from his upbringing and education a regard for Prussia and Protestantism as the standard-bearers and motive forces of German ideals and achievements. This regard was to be tempered later when he came into contact with the Catholic south of Europe on his first visit to Portugal and Spain.

The comfortable *fin de siècle* world of Baden-Baden collapsed with the outbreak of war in 1914. Forty years later Schneider recalled that summer in one of his autobiographical sketches, claiming that it was in the hotel, its façade decorated with the flags of all the European countries, that he first became aware of the unity of Europe (though there is probably here an element of distortion induced by hindsight). It was in the hotel, too, that he experienced the catastrophe of the collapse of Europe, with the hasty and tearful departure of Russian, French and other guests, now enemies.

Whatever the effect of the First World War on Europe, it brought ruin to Schneider's family. The hotel could not be saved and had to be sold. Shortly afterwards, in 1922, Schneider's father took his own life. Schneider himself, who might have looked forward to a relatively cushioned existence, had to abandon any thought of attending university and was obliged to earn his living. After a disastrous year attempting to become a farmer, he moved to Dresden, where he stayed for seven years, earning a precarious living translating the foreign-language correspondence of a picture postcard firm.

These were years of great privation, not just for Schneider. The early 1920s were years of disastrous inflation and political instability in Germany. If the period between 1924 and 1929 seemed to bring a fragile prosperity and stability, the battle-lines had long been drawn and with the Wall Street Crash of late 1929 the way was opened for the rise of the Third Reich. Despite privations so great that his health was permanently affected, Schneider undertook a vast programme of self-education, reading most of the great Western philosophers and other European writers, especially German writers. Of particular significance were the Greek tragedies and the writings of Plato, Shakespeare, Whitman, Kierkegaard, Schopenhauer, Nietzsche and Unamuno. As well as immersing himself in philosophy and literature he extended his knowledge of European languages: English, French, Italian, Spanish, Portuguese and, later, Danish. The erudition acquired by this autodidactic ascesis is evident in his writings.

The immediate stimulus to that educational effort was the failure of a suicide attempt which he made shortly after his father's death in 1922. After his attempt on his life he felt what he called a "burning desire for the life of the spirit".[1] But until his death, and certainly from the time he became a Christian, Schneider was haunted by what he regarded as this great sin. Importantly too, "the inner wound it leaves does not heal. Whoever has cut himself off in this way from the world and his fellow men will never again sit at their table with undivided heart."[2] As another important consequence of this unsuccessful suicide attempt, he was virtually adopted by his landlady, Anna Maria Baumgarten, twenty years his senior. The nineteen-year-old was taken into her care and lived with her until his death thirty-six years later. They never married.

A small legacy which resulted from the belated winding-up of his father's affairs enabled Schneider to spend the winter of 1928–29 in Portugal and Spain. It was from this time that he dated his career as a writer. It was also at this time that he began to travel extensively in Europe. At first these travels were mainly in the south of Europe but, even before the War, he twice visited England. After the interruption caused by the Second World War, he resumed his travels, developing a keen interest in Scandinavia. A firm believer in the "feel" or atmosphere of place, Schneider tried for the rest of his life to visit as many as possible of the places in Europe that figured in his writings, particularly in his historical ones.

Schneider's life and work as a writer may be divided into three phases. The first (*circa* 1928–38) is dominated initially by a tragic nihilism which develops into a conviction that history is tragedy under the Cross. The middle period (1938–51 *circa*) is characterized by Christian belief and a fight against the Third Reich, and after 1945 by criticism of what he saw as the German failure or refusal to face up to the lessons of that Reich. The third and final phase, from about 1951 to his death in 1958, is marked by the crucified Christ of Golgotha, by the theology of the Cross and, especially towards the end, by a profound crisis of personal confidence in his own faith and world-view. While throughout his life Schneider wrote novels, drama, poetry, essays and historical monographs, each phase is marked by a preference for one or more of these forms. His first phase is dominated by literary studies of poets, monarchs and other historical persons and institutions. In his second phase he preferred the essay, the short meditation, and above all the sonnet form. In his third phase, while the essay remained conspicuous, he turned to drama and, in his last five years, to autobiography.

Of crucial importance to Schneider, together with his failed suicide attempt, was his reading, in 1926, of Miguel de Unamuno's *Del sentimiento tragico de la vida*. Of this Schneider wrote: "It was not the philosophy that convinced me [...]. In my inner pain, it was the idea of existence as death-struggle, as passionate battle with time, as incessant challenge, that stirred me, consoled me, confirmed me."[3] But in 1926 he had not yet clarified his own expression of the tragic character of human living. Nor had he begun to examine the manifestation of the tragic in the history of individuals and societies. He had only just begun that pilgrimage that was to take him, via his experiences of Spain and Portugal (experiences both of the countries themselves and of their literatures), through an understanding and love of Christianity (particularly Catholicism) as a cultural and historical phenomenon, to a personal religious commitment. This pilgrimage was hastened by Schneider's experience of the rise of the Nazi Party and of the first two years of the Third Reich, and ended in early 1937 with his return to the practice of Catholicism.

For Schneider, 1929–38 was a period of consciously literary and in some cases very lengthy studies of figures in literature and history who incarnated for him his developing views on the role of the tragic in history and in the lives of individuals and nations. In a series of studies embracing Camões, Pombal, Philip II of Spain, Fichte, the Hohenzollerns, the British Empire and finally, in 1937–38, Bartolomé de Las Casas, Schneider developed his views on the nature and role of the state, of monarchy, of power and its use and effects, of religion, of physical and mental suffering, of sacrifice and inevitable failure as constitutive realities of all living. The tragic nihilism he had found in Unamuno complemented in his mind what he called the gentle atheism of Schopenhauer, a writer in whom he had found an interpreter of and companion in his own suffering, and who had made possible a solidarity with fellow sufferers, that is, with all creatures. Schneider's contact with the Catholic south of Europe, and in particular with the mysticism of Teresa of Avila and John of the Cross, began to lead him in the direction of a personal religious commitment. An equally important thrust came from his interpretation not only of European history but also of the rise of various right-wing tendencies in Germany, of which the Nazi Party was only the most extreme. That rise, and with it the eventual accession to power of Adolf Hitler, caused Schneider to question the validity of the theories of the third great influence on his earlier period, Friedrich Nietzsche.

From the time he was a boy Schneider had been a monarchist, and he remained one all his life. For most of the 1920s and 1930s he shared some of the restorationist aspirations of many of his background and class and, for several years, was an admirer of what he saw as the Prussian ideal. In the mid-1930s he even became friendly with the former Kaiser Wilhelm II and with the Crown Prince. But, even by then, he had begun to question the feasibility and desirability of a restoration of the monarchy and to doubt the possibility of any earthly incarnation of his imperial ideal: an imperial ideal which was becoming increasingly that of the Kingdom of God could not be realized in a world without God. If he had previously hoped for the restoration of a tragically self-sacrificing monarch, he gradually came to believe that the tragic, self-sacrificial, self-destructive exercise of power could be entrusted only to a monarch who was divinely sanctioned, a monarch patterned on the crucified Christ.

The emergence of the anti-monarch, Adolf Hitler, in the early months of 1933 led Schneider to see in Nietzsche the logical term of a development which had begun at the latest with Lessing in the eighteenth century and continued through Kant, Fichte, Hegel, and Schelling. For Schneider this development, starting from the abandonment of Christ as divine, led through the abandonment of truth, via a morality based on duty, to the abandonment of religion and God, and with them the abandonment of conscience, and on to the sacrifice of the individual and the delivery of whole peoples to the demands of an all-powerful state and the dictates of one man's will-to-power. In Schneider's view the history of the previous 150 years in Germany had been that of the progressive and disastrous abandonment of what he saw as Germany's paradigmatic role as the embodiment of the European destiny and ideal—a tragic striving beyond the limitations of human living, a doomed attempt to incarnate the Kingdom of God on earth. In simplistic terms, Nietzsche led to Hitler, therefore the line of thought that led to Nietzsche must be re-examined, while Hitler and all he stood for were to be resisted.

But if Schneider abandoned Nietzsche he held fast to the fundamental insight he had gained from Unamuno. All life, all history, is essentially tragic, essentially bound to fail; but it is now a failure in the shadow of the saving Cross of the crucified Christ. The immortality, the next life that Unamuno longed for but could not affirm, is proclaimed by Schneider to be the resolution, if on another plane, of the tragedy inherent in existence. The gentle atheism and love of fellow sufferers that Schneider had learned from Schopenhauer are transformed into a Franciscan concern for all creation.

So much attention has been given to the first phase of Schneider's life as a writer because there is not a single theme in his later writings that has not been treated or at least adumbrated in this phase. True, emphases differ in the later phases, and there remains the problem of understanding Schneider's shift in content while he continued to use the same vocabulary. To the end, though, Schneider thought and wrote in dualities—though not necessarily always in opposites. There is a thematic consistency in the development and sequence of his three phases. Constantly recurring are Portuguese *saudade* and Unamuno's *hambre del immortalidad*, chaos and the will to form, idyll and destruction, empire and crown, kingship and renunciation, struggle and resistance to dictatorship, power and guilt, prayer and consolation, bios and cosmos, decay and suffering, peace and the eschaton, office and charism, the Sermon on the Mount and Christian radicalism, dissonance and anarchy, northern European piety and southern European desire for tragedy, tragedy under the Cross and religious utopianism. And over all, especially in his last phase, hovers the shadow of death. Caught as he was between his inherited melancholy and unconditional acceptance of the Cross, it was in the perspective of death that Schneider placed the question of the meaning of life.

Schneider's first phase came to an end in March 1938 with the completion of *Las Casas vor Karl v*, understood by him and many others as an attack on the persecution of the Jews. (This is one of the few books by Schneider to have been translated into English: it was published in New York in 1948 under the title *Imperial Mission*.) Indeed, as early as 29 November 1933, prompted by first reports of the existence of concentration camps in Germany, he had written the story "Der Tröster" ["The Consoler"], in which he examined the attitudes and activities of the Jesuit Friedrich Spee von Langenfeld in the pastoral care of so-called condemned witches in the early seventeenth century. This story was Schneider's first act of "literary" protest against a Nazi regime with which, after initial hopes that it might be the vehicle of national revival, he had become rapidly disillusioned. His study of the Hohenzollerns, published in 1933, made it clear that he considered Nazism a perversion of the Prussian ideal, and it was duly suppressed. A similar fate befell two later books, *Das Inselreich* ["The Island Empire"] (1939), his study of the British Empire, and *Kaiser Lothars Krone* ["Emperor Lothar's Crown"] (1937), both of which were attacked in the Nazi newspaper *Völkische Beobachter* on 5 March 1938. Nevertheless, as late as 1940, when *Macht und Gnade* ["Power and Grace"], a collection of historical essays, appeared, Schneider was able to publish legally. Attempts were made, however, to hinder the appearance of his work by means of paper rationing. Finally, in 1941, the Ministry of Propaganda officially forbade the printing and publication of further books by Schneider. From this time until the end of the War he would publish semi-legally or illegally with the help of friends, among whom the most important was Joseph Rossé, owner of the Alsatia publishing firm at Colmar in Alsace. *Macht und Gnade* contained forty-seven essays, some of which had been written as early as 1934. Schneider's first essay to be published, "Corneilles Ethos in der Ära Ludwig xiv", appeared on 15 September 1939. For the next ten years, until the publication of his political drama *Der Kronprinz* in 1948, the essay was to be his most formal mode of addressing his readers.

But if, because of government prohibitions, Schneider had to wait until after the War for the essay to become a more effective vehicle, he developed another form with which to reach a wider reading public. As early as 1940, he had taken a conscious decision to cease all purely literary activity and concentrate on what he called *Sanitätsdienst*, or first aid. Unfit for military service on health grounds, he understood his role as one of providing consolation and encouragement to soldiers and a general public oppressed by the regime and by the realities of the War. By means of privately printed pamphlets—short meditations on religious themes, lives of the saints and historical figures—, Schneider sought not only to console but to keep alive the awareness of spiritual and religious alternatives to the Nazi system, to preserve an awareness of Germany's belonging to a wider European tradition, and, increasingly, to prepare for the post-Nazi period: despite his ingrained pessimism he never doubted the defeat of the regime. But it was above all in his sonnets, hundreds of which circulated in what are now calculated to have been several hundred thousand duplicated and hand-copied pamphlets, that his voice was heard. He chose the sonnet deliberately as the embodiment of strict form in an era without form.

Another important aspect of Schneider's *Sanitätsdienst* was his voluminous correspondence with soldiers at the front, many of whom were in profound crisis of conscience because of what they had seen and been ordered to do. The quantity of this correspondence became so great that Schneider was unable even to open, let alone read, the letters he received. This correspondence placed him under constant suspicion by the Gestapo, to the extent that he had to burn the letters not destroyed when his house was bombed in 1944. The illegal publication of some of his sonnets and meditations in occupied Poland led Martin Bormann, early in 1945, to order Schneider's arrest for treason. Schneider escaped the Gestapo only because he was in hospital waiting for an operation and in the confusion of the Allied invasion was forgotten.

During the War Schneider found his main sources of strength and inspiration in his personal Christian beliefs and membership of the Church. As the War progressed, leading to the collapse of Nazi rule, he became increasingly convinced that Christianity alone could provide the moral and intellectual foundations of reconstruction, primarily for Germany but also for the whole of Europe—the moral and intellectual underpinning of that individual responsibility and freedom which had been one of the major casualties of the Nazi system. Indeed, the destruction (and abdication) of individual responsibility and freedom had been one of the major causes of the inevitable collapse of that system.

For some three or four years after the collapse of 1945, Schneider continued to have, publicly, as considerable an influence in and on Christian literate and literary circles as he had had clandestinely during the War. In a flood of articles and essays, published under titles such as "Gedanken des Friedens" ["Thoughts of Peace"] (1946), "Macht des Geistes" ["The Power of the Spirit"] (1946) and "Das Erbe in Feuer" ["Inheritance in the Flames"] (1946), he pleaded and argued for an honest examination of and confrontation with German history, especially that of the recent past, and German possibilities in the light of Christian tradition and beliefs. "I really thought I saw a people on its way back to God," he wrote in *Verhüllter Tag.*[4] He was bitterly disappointed when such an examination and confrontation were submerged in the exigencies of economic and political reconstruction and, increasingly, of the Cold War. He questioned what he considered to be Germany's uncritical pursuit of economic recovery and development while it ignored and failed to come to terms with the political and moral disaster that had been the Third Reich. This ignoring and this failure by the political powers were reflected, for Schneider, in the relative ease with which the new state acquiesced to the division of Germany into two states, each dependent on one of the opposing superpowers, and the ease with which the Federal Republic accepted rearmament and eventually, by membership of NATO, the nuclear arms race. Schneider's criticism reflected his growing alienation from the developing West German state and its functionaries. (An exception was his friend Dr Theodor Heuss, the first Federal President, who was largely responsible for Schneider's "rehabilitation" in 1955–56.)[5] This criticism and this alienation were, in turn, to alienate or at least arouse the suspicions of many groups and individuals for whom Schneider had been an inspiration and consolation during the Second World War. Such groups and individuals were mystified and even angered by Schneider's occasional contributions to publications of the East German peace movement—the latter resulting from his contacts with Bertolt Brecht and Johannes R. Becher, the GDR Minister for Culture. He came to be regarded by many, especially by those of Christian sympathy, as a renegade prophet.

Alienation from the new state might have been personally disappointing for Schneider but, after the Third Reich, this experience was not new. More distressing for him than any distancing from the state and its institutions was his distancing from and the suspicion in which he was held by the hierarchy of the Roman Catholic Church in Germany. In addition, that suspicion had economic consequences, since much of Schneider's income came from occasional journalism, literary criticism and lecturing; and from 1951 to 1953 he found it impossible to gain access to Catholic newspapers and journals. Throughout this period rumours were current in Catholic circles of Schneider's defection from the Church and adherence to Communism. Economic considerations apart, Schneider was caused great mental suffering by what he regarded as the unholy alliance between the Roman Catholic Church and the new Federal Republic. He was distressed most particularly by the close contacts he saw between the Church and the Christian Democratic Union. Schneider saw such contacts as a betrayal of what he considered to be the Church's role, namely, that of champion, even guarantor, of the rights and responsibilities of individual conscience, of personal freedom and, despite the Church's own failings, as a counterweight to the power of an overweening state. When Schneider was awarded the Peace Prize of the German Book Trade at Frankfurt's Paulskirche in 1956, this honour was regarded by many as the culmination of a series of acts of public rehabilitation and restitution by the Federal Republic of Germany. But Schneider never considered himself to be in need of rehabilitation and never retracted any of his written or spoken utterances. In the years 1951–55, most particularly from 1951 to

1953, he was an uncomfortable and unwelcome critic of the new West German state.

Schneider was led to his third phase as a writer by the disappointment of his hope that in post-war Germany it might be possible to build a new society based on the ideals of freedom, conscience, personal responsibility to the truth, genuine peace, Christian values, an awareness of the tragic nature of human and societal existence and the need for grace. Abandoning the hope of the incarnation of these ideals by any existing institution—considering that impossibility, indeed, as one further manifestation of the tragic—, he turned to the individual. His first play had been published in 1948, but from 1950 onwards he published a series of plays, in which all his familiar themes were presented, most usually in the form of a confrontation of the individual with institutions and their representatives. Thus he presents a dramatized version of the confrontation between Las Casas and Charles V, a theme already treated in his book of 1938; he presents the confrontation between Innocent III and Francis of Assisi, the election and resignation of Celestine V, the personality of Alexander I of Russia. In all these plays the decisive element is the necessary clash between opposites and the destructive effect on individuals of the necessary exercise of power. While Schneider was aware of his deficiencies as a playwright, and was pleased and flattered when his plays were performed and even won awards, he seems to have intended these plays primarily for the reading public. Significantly, the public success of some of them came after Schneider's period of "disgrace" between 1951 and 1953.

Prompted by what he regarded as an idealized and inaccurate biography of him published to mark his fiftieth birthday in 1953 by the Swiss theologian Hans Urs von Balthasar, Schneider turned to a genre he had hitherto dismissed. He had made one or two autobiographical sketches for an edition of his selected works, but he now turned in earnest to setting the record straight. In the resulting autobiography, *Verhüllter Tag* ["The Shrouded Day"] (1954), there are already hints of the collapse that was to become apparent in the diary he kept of his last winter, 1957–58, which he spent in Vienna: entitled *Winter in Wien*, it was published towards the end of 1958, after his death. His disillusionment with the institutions of state and Church had led not only to a preoccupation with the individual and his role *vis-à-vis* those institutions, but also to a radical questioning of his own faith and world-view. Schneider himself did not doubt that his own personality and his poor health contributed to the questioning documented in this book, which is actually a series of autobiographical, historical, philosophical, theological and literary meditations. The book not only covers the complete range of Schneider's themes, but opens up a new and, to many of his readers, terrifying perspective.

The collapse documented in *Winter in Wien* cannot be described or dismissed simply as a loss of faith or withdrawal of belief. There would seem to be more to the process than a descent into despair and agnostic *aporia* by a disappointed and redundant prophet. It is still unclear how, if at all, the collapse, described by Schneider himself as "ein innerer Unfall" ["an accident inside myself"] and "dieses Herausgleiten aus jeglichem Horizont" ["this slipping out of every perspective"],[6] is to be explained and interpreted. What is certain is that Schneider's apparent radicalism, not least his apparent inability to affirm the Resurrection, was deeply shocking to many of those readers for whom Schneider had been prophet and interpreter for nearly two decades. It was clear that despite the apparent rehabilitation of 1956 disagreements were deeper than ever. Death, which could be glimpsed through all Schneider's writings, seemed to have triumphed—death seen as the original darkness, eternal nothingness, chaos, cruel God, eternal sleep, Christian Cross; death the darkened sun under which life shines eerily, blossoms effusively, then decays; death as "grief for the creature and for the hidden God".[7] In death the mystery of the crucified Christ of Golgotha is resolved. For Schneider there remains only prayer, prayer beyond belief. And meanwhile God is death, and death is God and the nothingness of the mystics.[8]

Reinhold Schneider died on Easter Sunday, 6 April 1958, as a result of injuries received in a fall while returning from a visit to church on Easter Saturday, just five days after he had submitted the manuscript of *Winter in Wien*.

## NOTES

1   R. Schneider, *Verhüllter Tag*, in his *Gesammelte Werke*, vol. x, edited by J. Rast (Frankfurt-on-Main, Insel, 1978), p. 49.

2   R. Schneider, *Verhüllter Tag*, p. 51.

3   R. Schneider, *Verhüllter Tag*, p. 52.

4    R. Schneider, *Verhüllter Tag*, p. 144.

5    That action by Heuss seems to have been both a response to urgings by friends of Schneider, not least Werner Bergengruen, and a personal act of friendship. (This was suggested to me by Heinrich Ludewig in a conversation of 28 July 1991.)

6    R. Schneider, *Winter in Wien*, in his *Gesammelte Werke*, vol. x, pp. 233, 264.

7    R. Schneider, *Winter in Wien*, p. 405.

8    See E. Blattmann, *Reinhold Schneider Linguistisch Interpretiert* = vol. II of *Literatur Linguistik Didaktik: Beiträge zu Theorie und Praxis* (Heidelberg, Stiehm, 1979), p. 11.

# YEATS AND HEANEY:
## DANTE AS AUTHOR AND GUIDE

*Hugh Prior*

When we consider Yeats's relationship to Dante the poet, or more accurately to his idea of Dante the poet, "the chief imagination of Christendom" as he calls him in "Ego Dominus Tuus", we see an approach to life and art that is kinetic rather than static.[1] That Yeats should choose "Ego Dominus Tuus" as the title for a poem of 1915 that enacts, as well as meditating upon, the dialectical nature of the artist is indicative of the deep sympathy in which he felt himself to be with Dante as a poet. "Ego dominus tuus" comes from the *Vita nuova*, that strange and beautiful account of Dante's developing poetic consciousness. The phrase is enunciated to the poet, as the *Vita nuova* relates, in a vision. Significantly, in his essay "Per Amica Silentia Lunae" Yeats focuses on this. "At times," he writes, "I remember that place in Dante where he sees in his chamber the 'Lord of Terrible aspect', and how, seeming to 'rejoice inwardly that it was a marvel to see', speaking, he said many things among which I could understand but few, and of these, this: ego dominus tuus..."[2]

"That place in Dante", as Yeats puts it, is Chapter 3 of the *Vita nuova*. Dante there describes "una maravigliosa visione" in which, rather dramatically, he is shown his heart—"Vide cor tuum."[3] What is significant to Yeats is the idea that, to develop fully, a poet's consciousness is open to, and requires as external agency, a guide or anti-self—an anti-self because this guide, or lord as in the *Vita nuova*, is the antithesis of the poet's native disposition. Such antithesis is betokened by Dante's description: "una figura d'uno segnore di pauroso aspetto". Yeats elaborates on this artistic dialectic, on how the creative imagination finds its true course "through antithetical emotion", in phase seventeen of *A Vision*. Phase seventeen deals with the instance of what Yeats calls "Daimonic Man", of which he cites

Dante as one prominent example. And it is highly likely that Yeats
also considered himself to belong to this phase. To fulfil his potential
an artist born into phase seventeen must do as Dante did, according
to Yeats, that is, adopt the "Mask of Simplicity that is also intensity".[4]

This antithetical process is what Yeats describes in the dialogic
poem "Ego Dominus Tuus" with reference to Dante and to Keats.
According to Yeats the image of Dante that we receive as "so utterly
[...] himself"—

> that hollow face of his
> More plain to the mind's eye than any face
> But that of Christ

—is really an antithetical mask, "a simplification through intensity"
that liberated Dante from the "dispersal" of his lustful nature and its
desires, not the least of which was his desire for Beatrice ("A hunger
for the apple on the bough/Most out of reach"). Dante, through his
mask, and not through the native form of his selfhood—in Yeats's
words—"found the unpersuadable justice, he found/The most exalted lady loved by man." In other words, for Yeats Dante's gaunt,
ascetic aspect is the antithesis of the flesh and blood man. Dante
elevates sensual desire to the vision of spiritual love and is able to
accomplish his great poetic achievement because he adopts such a
mask.

Rather than succumbing to his own native disposition, says
Yeats in *A Vision*, Dante "attained, as poet, to Unity of Being, as poet
saw all things set in order, had an intellect that served the Mask alone,
that compelled even those things that opposed it to serve, and was
content to see both good and evil."[5] Yeats's repetition of the phrase
"as poet" is important. He held the view that, as he put it in his
*Memoirs*, there is a great distinction "between the artistic and the
daily self". While Yeats's reference to unity of being might seem to
offer ultimate stasis, his systematizing vision is dynamic in its
historical antitheses and in its elevations and sublimations of personal experience. So too Dante's universe operates upon the dynamic of *amore*, or love, a force which can also turn in antithetical
distortion to evil.

Yeats's experience as a poet may be seen to connect with Dante's
in many important ways. Both loved an unattainable woman and
both were visited by what each termed visions. Indeed, Yeats
described the patterns of *A Vision* as "stylistic arrangements of

experience",[6] which is surely not an inappropriate description of Dante's *Vita nuova*. There is at the core of Yeats's approach to Dante the idea of a poet's need for vision and for guidance. This same need is evidenced in Dante himself—in his elevation of Beatrice and in his employment of Virgil as "duca" and "maestro" in the first two *cantiche* of the *Commedia*. Implicit in all this is the felt problematic of the poet as author, claiming, requiring and availing himself of authority.

This problem of the authority of the author also emerges in Seamus Heaney's connections with Dante. It is hardly to be wondered at that a poet who has had a brilliant career, in terms of both its productivity and the acclaim it has deservedly received, should search uneasily for responsibility and authority when that same poet comes from a place stricken by political violence, and when the growth of his reputation has been contemporaneous with the continuation of that violence. Heaney's poetry is frequently alerted by an awareness of being on the edge of division: division between the pressing demands of a personal lyric impulse born of a strong sense of native place, and the demand to address the political horrors of that poetic place which is also the place of history. To authenticate himself as a poet, surely Heaney must be responsible to his deepest lyric instincts; but to do this is also to lack responsibility (and thereby lose authority) because it seems unjustifiably hedonistic in the face of the atrocities erupting daily in Northern Ireland. Heaney has said:

> What I first loved in the *Commedia* was the local intensity, the vehemence and fondness attaching to individual shades, the way personalities and values were emotionally soldered together [...]. The way in which Dante could place himself in an historical world yet submit that world to scrutiny from a perspective beyond history [...].[7]

What Heaney says here implies much of what may explain why Dante, in particular, should attract the attention of Irish writers, namely, the need to recognize and negotiate history, in order to escape or transcend it. This is not a new imperative in Irish writing, and calls to mind the figure of Stephen Dedalus.

"The Strand at Lough Beg", in the collection *Field Work*, is an example of how Heaney enlists Dante's help in formulating a personal response to the sectarian murder of his second cousin which is also a response to the ultra-personal conditions that provoked such a brutal act of political conflict. The poem's last section takes the form of a dreamlike evocation of the poet and his cousin Colum McCartney, walking, in a procession reminiscent of Dante and Virgil, through the morning mists on the shores of Lough Beg. Heaney beautifully evokes here an ethereal sense of transition from the actual. But this ethereal tranquillity is broken in the poignant gesture of the poet stooping over the murdered body of his cousin:

> I turn
> because the sweeping of your feet
> has stopped behind me, to find you
> on your knees with blood in your hair and eyes.[8]

Then, re-enacting Virgil's cleansing of Dante's face of the taints of Hell in *Purgatorio* I, Heaney's poem concludes:

> Then kneel in front of you in brimming grass
> And gather up cold handfuls of the dew
> To wash you, cousin. I dab you clean with moss
> Fine as the drizzle out of a low cloud.
> I lift you under the arms and lay you flat.
> With rushes that shoot green again, I plait
> Green scapulars to wear over your shroud.

The awful sense of personal loss—intensified by the manner in which that loss was inflicted—is rendered by expression of the psychic need both to address and to redress the fact of death through healing rites. But, beyond this personal dimension, the poem is also an expression of a collective woundedness, and of the sense of a need for some redemptive element (here Dante's rush) that can outface the brutality of such murder. The nexus in which these personal and socio-political dimensions converge is the Dantean prologue that Heaney gives the poem with his translation of lines 100–03 of *Purgatorio* I:

> All round this little island, on the strand
> Far down below there, where the breakers strive,
> Grow the tall rushes from the oozy sand.

The image of the island buffeted by waves speaks to Ireland beset by the agonies of sectarian politics. Dante's humble, cleansing rush betokens the small, the ordinary: something which in its very humility becomes a talisman that can erase the marks of Hell. And Hell here is contemporary Irish history. The danger, however, is that poetry aestheticizes such instances: that while poetry as expression exposes such raw agonies, poetry as work of composition betrays those agonies into aesthetic composure.

Heaney faces this very issue, once again using Dantean gestures to enable him to do so, in section eight of *Station Island*. Here, in the island setting of St Patrick's Purgatory, Heaney was himself confronted by the spirit of that same murdered second cousin:

> And so I pleaded with my second cousin
> "I kept seeing a grey stretch of Lough Beg
> and the strand empty at daybreak.
> I felt like the bottom of a dried up lake."[9]

And Heaney has his cousin's ghost reply:

> You saw that and you wrote that, not the fact.
> You confused evasion with artistic tact.

The apparition goes on to challenge the poet,

> for the way you whitewashed ugliness and drew
> the lovely blinds of the Purgatorio
> and saccharined my death with morning dew.

The question of the poet's authority, authenticity and responsibility, and of the whole business of poetry, is here raised explicitly. These troubling issues, however, are also discernible in the earlier collection *Field Work*, and it is significant that Heaney invokes Dante in those instances too. In "An Afterwards" he says of his wife:

> She would plunge all poets in the ninth circle
> And fix them, tooth in skull, tonguing brain.

The ninth circle of Hell is where Dante locates Ugolino, cannibalistically feasting upon Archbishop Ruggieri. Indeed, *Field Work* concludes with Heaney's own translation of the Ugolino episode in Cantos XXXII and XXXIII of *Inferno*. The alignment of poets with a damned figure such as Ugolino suggests that Heaney is morally sensitive to the voracious aspect of the poet's enterprise. Poets, as it were, eat up human experience to feed the purposes of their art. Yet the very sensitivity to this, and the expression of it, bespeak a desire to establish a moral authority for the authorial role.

The burden of such sensitivity and such a desire is, I believe, the deep-rooted impetus that drives Heaney to connect with Dante. For Dante's self-presentation in the *Commedia* comprehends and, in a qualified way, resolves this problem of authority.

The very fact that Dante casts himself as a unique pilgrim privileged to obtain a view of the afterlife and the ordering of justice would seem, in itself, to constitute a claim to authority. But Dante authenticates such authoritative status by marking the difficulty of its attainment, and expresses this difficulty as both a technical one—the search for an adequate poetic language and register—and one which is a test and proof of personal integrity and moral courage. This form of authentication is established in the very first canto of the *Commedia*:

> Ahi quanto a dir qual era è cosa dura
> esta selva selvaggia e aspra e forte
> che nel pensier rinova la paura![10]

Dante presents himself as someone at a loss, struggling towards comprehension and expression. It is this very sense of struggle, of the experience and its translation into verse being hard-earned, that authenticates Dante's great poem. It is, paradoxically, Dante's authorial deficiency that renders his authority efficient. And this mode of self-presentation is reinforced by Dante's choice of Virgil as guiding author: "Tu se' lo mio maestro e 'l mio autore" is what Dante says to Virgil in *Inferno*.[11] Virgil is a model both of authorial authority and of its limitation. It is this same mode of self-presentation that Heaney adopts in *Station Island*, thereby gaining a qualified but authenticated authority.

## NOTES

1   W. B. Yeats, *The Poems*, edited by D. Albright (London, Dent, 1990), pp. 210–12.

2   W. B. Yeats, *A Vision and Related Writings*, selected and edited by A. N. Jeffares (London, Arena, 1990), p. 96.

3   *Vita nuova*, edited by D. De Robertis, in Dante Alighieri, *Opere minori*, 2 vols in 3 (Milan–Naples, Ricciardi, 1979–88), I, i, 27–247 (pp. 37–39).

4   W. B. Yeats, *A Vision*, p. 174.

5   W. B. Yeats, *A Vision*, p. 174.

6   See B. L. Croft's *"Stylistic Arrangement of Experience"* (London, Bucknell University Press, 1987) for an examination of *A Vision*.

7   Seamus Heaney, "Envies and Identifications: Dante and the Modern Poet", in *Dante Readings*, edited by E. Haywood (Dublin, Irish Academic Press, 1987), pp. 29–46 (p. 45).

8   Seamus Heaney, *Field Work* (London, Faber, 1979), pp. 17–18.

9   Seamus Heaney, *Station Island* (London, Faber, 1984), p. 83.

10  Dante Alighieri, *La "Commedia" secondo l'antica vulgata*, edited by G. Petrocchi, second revised reprint, 4 vols (Florence, Le Lettere, 1994), II, 3–4 (*Inferno*, I. 4–6).

11  Dante Alighieri, *La "Commedia"*, II, 14 (*Inferno*, I. 85).

# "ENTRE LE GALET ET LA MER": READING A BECKETT POEM BETWEEN TWO LANGUAGES

## Patricia Coughlan

je suis ce cours de sable qui glisse
entre le galet et la dune
la pluie d'été pleut sur ma vie
sur moi ma vie qui me fuit me poursuit
et finira le jour de son commencement

cher instant je te vois
dans ce rideau de brume qui recule
où je n'aurai plus à fouler ces longs seuils mouvants
et vivrai le temps d'une porte
qui s'ouvre et se referme

my way is in the sand flowing
between the shingle and the dune
the summer rain rains on my life
on me my life harrying fleeing
to its beginning to its end

my peace is there in the receding mist
when I may cease from treading these long shifting thresholds
and live the space of a door
that opens and shuts

1948[1]

[...] an infinity [...] which, after the loss of a transcendental economy of salvation and return, can manifest itself only in the form of Hegel's *bad infinity*: as the thorn of yearning woven or driven into discourse, and as the boundlessness of being underway, without an absolute goal.[2]

Beckett's poem "je suis ce cours de sable qui glisse" was first published in the post-war special issue of the magazine *transition*, which was edited by Georges Duthuit in 1948. Accompanied by two other brief pieces, entitled "que ferais-je dans ce monde sans visage sans questions"/"what would I do in this world faceless incurious" and "je voudrais que mon amour meure"/"I would like my love to die", it appeared in French and English, the two versions on facing pages. The poem has not attracted much commentary, though critics who have discussed it agree about its outstanding quality. Marjorie Perloff borrows the phrase "the space of a door" from its penultimate line for a chapter title in her study *The Poetics of Indeterminacy: Rimbaud to Cage*, and discerns in it the dream sequences of *How It Is* "existing in embryo". She finds the oddity of "the door, enigmatically planted on the empty beach" to be a classic instance of deferral, a simultaneous offering and withholding of meaning.[3] Lawrence Harvey also briefly discusses the poem, comparing some elements of the French and English versions and, unlike Perloff, finding the English one superior.[4] The present essay examines the poem more closely, as a particularly eloquent articulation, in a small compass, of Beckett's thought in the period. My purpose is especially to explore the interpretative possibilities, or chinks, offered by the fact of the poem's two versions and their small disparities: wrinkles, flaws, tiny folds or scratches in its smooth and enigmatic surface, offering a little purchase in the reader's scramble towards the interpretation of a particularly recalcitrant work. The very existence of the twin texts may also be taken as an instance of the way Beckett's imagination always tends to dualities and generally leaves them unreconciled.

Let us begin by looking at their temporal context in Beckett's work. In January 1948 he had finished *Molloy*, the first novel of the trilogy, and during the same year he was working on *Malone Dies*, the second. In 1946 he had completed the four *nouvelles*, of which *L'Expulsé* and *Premier Amour* are the best known, and also the novel *Mercier et Camier*. Besides these fictions and others, he also wrote during these years some important pieces of criticism, in particular, in 1948 itself, the essay *Peintres de l'empêchement*. In this piece, as elsewhere, he praises the work of the Dutch brother painters Abraham and Gerard van Velde as paradigm examples of modern art; but, as with his other art criticism, the discussion is of intense primary interest to interpreters of Beckett's own work.

At the beginning of the essay Beckett sardonically pretends to be seeking a clear and simple "formula" to define modern art, and thus to pin it down. He affects to be resisting any notion of overdetermination in aesthetic phenomena, or of indeterminacy in their interpretation. In this passage we find him using what is one of the governing metaphors of our poem. Ironically propounding a wish for certainty in criticism by means of adopting a fixed "formula" for characterizing acceptable art, he says:

> Savoir ce qu'on veut dire, voilà la sagesse. Et le meilleur moyen de savoir ce qu'on veut dire, c'est de vouloir dire la même chose tous les jours, avec patience, et de se familiariser ainsi avec la formule employée, dans tous ses sables mouvants.

> [Knowing what you want to say, that is wisdom. And the best way of knowing what you want to say is to want to say the same thing every day, patiently, and thus to familiarise yourself with the chosen formula, with all its shifting sands.][5]

What, if anything, can we make of this coincidence of metaphorical language? Beckett's position in the essay would appear to be that even a "formula" would not definitively pin down the character of modern art, and that a formula would itself escape determinacy and the control of its very proponents. So we may say that while the poem presents a state of radical uncertainty and flux which, taken in isolation, we would be likely to understand as a psychological matter—reading the signals of the solitary speaker within the conventions of the lyric—the prose piece describes the condition of critics, would-be users of discursive and authoritative language, as one of equal shiftingness, both before the phenomenon they are attempting to describe and in the formulation of their own thought.

I shall return explicitly to the preoccupation with indeterminacy. Meanwhile, another passage in the critical essay provides an even more striking gloss on the poem. Beckett finds in the two brothers' work two different but matching processes. In Gerard's art he discerns "un dévoilement sans fin, voile derrière voile, plan sur plan de transparences imparfaites, un dévoilement vers l'indévoilable, le rien, la chose à nouveau [an endless unveiling, veil behind veil, plane after plane of near-transparencies, and unveiling towards that which cannot be unveiled: nothing, the thing all over again]", while in Abraham's work there is "l'ensevelissment dans l'unique, dans un lieu d'impénétrables proximités, cellule peinte sur la pierre de la cellule, art d'incarcération [burial in the singular, in a place of impenetrable proximities, a cell painted on the stones of a cell, the art of incarceration]" (p. 136). These descriptions with their different metaphors invoke a process of infinite regress: just as the cherished moment, the "peace" desired by the speaker, can only be fruitlessly sought "in the receding mist", so the two painters and their respective audiences are ceaselessly drawn onwards towards an ever-receding revelation, or shut inside the monadic cell of perceptual repetition.

If at this stage we propose provisionally to define the poem's theme, we may say that it concerns liminality, a condition of being set at a border, neither sea nor land. The word "seuils/thresholds" expresses it well. It explores the instability of the self: made of sand and/or made of water: neither definite. Sand is not cohesive: it crumbles, absorbs water, and, of course, shifts. There is a difficulty in making prose sense of the first line, a difficulty exacerbated—no doubt intentionally on Beckett's part—by the ambiguity of the verb "suis" in the French version: "I am" or "I follow".[6] That is, either the speaker *is* a kind of river of sand (itself a paradoxical notion) or he *follows* one. The English—"my way is in the sand flowing"—is no less unresolved: what is it that flows, the sand or the "way"? This opening statement thus gives the impression of the self as something never finished, of its perpetual indefiniteness. The sand, the summer rain (line 3), and the mist (lines 6, 7) are all traditional images of transience.

Like most of Beckett's other poetry (except perhaps the Chamfort translations, *Huit Maximes*), this poem is studiedly non-discursive; generalizations, or anything in the nature of a sententious summing-up, in the manner of the solitary-self-in-nature meditations at the centre of the lyric since Romanticism, are withheld. We have only the beach-scape, if indeed we have that. As I have said, Perloff apprehends the "door" at the end as surrealist, "enigmatically planted on an empty beach", in the manner of Magritte, and quite correctly remarks that in the poem "Beckett's dream images refuse to divulge what he called a 'notion'" (pages 246–47). The poem might be said to be nearly all vehicle, and scarcely at all tenor (as in I. A. Richards's theory); or rather, a straightforward distinction between tenor and vehicle cannot here be made.[7] The only approach to the provision of a "tenor" seems to be in lines 3–5 and the corresponding penultimate line, with their necessarily generalizing references to "ma vie/my life" and "où je [...] vivrai/when I may [...] live". One might put it another way and say that if we were to treat the poem as a narrative text, we should say that it is all scene and no summary. In this eschewing of a summing-up or vantage-point, the form of the poem mimics the theme of evanescence, with its absence of full stops, irregularity of metre and line-length, and ambiguity of syntax.

Appropriate too is a specific consideration of the differences between the French and English versions. At the end of the first stanza, the French version makes a definite, though quirky, statement that the speaker's life "finira le jour de son commencement [will end the day of its beginning]" while the English merely disposes the end and the beginning as a parallelism, without definite syntactic pinning-down: "to its beginning to its end". Further, in the first line the English is vaguer again: it chooses a participle rather than the finite statement of a relative clause: "flowing" versus "qui glisse". In line 4 the English is also more ambiguous, less definite, leaving the notions of "harrying" and "fleeing" to float, as it were, as participles which we may attach either to "the summer rain" or to "my life". The French ties them down in a relative clause, giving the more precise information that it is "*ma vie* qui me fuit me poursuit" (my italics).

In the French, the second stanza performs an address: an intense interpersonal exchange, suggesting to many readers an amorous encounter; a moment of high rhetoric, which is in turn carefully cancelled by the revelation that the fulfilment of this desire would be, precisely, the ultimate removal of agency—the lifting of the obligation to act at all—along with the state of duration which only prolongs yearning. In the English, the expression "my peace" is more diffuse, already having given up the possibility of action from the start. In the penultimate line "le temps d'une porte" becomes "the space of a door": this imaginative interchangeability of time with space recalls Beckett's account of the Proustian subject as one extended in time as though it were space.[8] In both cases, duration is problematic and causes pain; we should also recall how intensely the Proust essay renders the suffering caused by the near-impossibility of making the desiring subject coincide with the desired object. The misty recession of the beloved moment, of the speaker's peace, vividly recalls these passages.

In both versions the mist conceals, but paradoxically also contains, or perhaps intimates, the speaker's "peace", or his "cher instant". Are we to understand that as the mist recedes/retreats, instead of uncovering and making manifest the wished-for fulfilment it further removes it? Its recession would, thus, remove the "cher instant", which remains tantalizingly withheld. This figure reverses or cancels a whole topos or motif in Western religious and literary thought: the figure of truth as temporarily concealed behind the veil of appearances, a Christian theological and Platonic idea. But whereas in traditional versions an ultimate unveiling is most decidedly envisaged, when the *telos* or end of this world is reached, Beckett, characteristically, imagines no effective end to this withholding. The veil (here the mist) is never rolled away, nor, if it were, would there be anything behind it at all—but another form of postponement, as in the trilogy there is always another narrative, another author inventing another character, another other-self. We may here recall Beckett's own invocation in his early poem *Alba* of the specifically Dantean unveiling, a paradigm case of this topos. In this anti-*aubade* it is, characteristically, summoned only to be cancelled—what in Dante is a cosmic revelation is supplanted in Beckett by the woman's actual physical presence, experienced as a kind of anti-revelation:

> whose beauty shall be a sheet before me
> a statement of itself drawn across the tempest of
> emblems
> so that there is no sun and no unveiling
> and no host
> only I and the sheet
> and bulk dead[9]

The beautiful passage detailing the endless unveilings—"voile derrière voile"—in Gerard van Velde's painting irresistibly reminds readers acquainted with post-structuralism of Derrida's infinite chain of signification, or what Umberto Eco calls endless semiosis, according to which every signifier suggests a signified, which is itself of course no more than another signifier with another signified beyond it, and so on, in a universe pullulating with meanings, as the trilogy pullulates with voices.[10] Barthes's famous coat-trailing manifesto for deconstructive interpretation in his 1968 essay "The Death of the Author" is appropriate:

> In the multiplicity of writing, everything is to be disentangled, nothing deciphered: the structure can be followed, "run" (like the thread of a stocking) at every point and at every level, but there is

nothing beneath: the space of writing is to be ranged over, not pierced; writing ceaselessly posits meaning ceaselessly to evaporate it, carrying out a systematic exemption of meaning;[11]

or, in Beckett's expression, an "empêchement".

In the poem before us, the essentially paradoxical quality of these formulations is represented by a peculiar temporal contradiction. More evident in the English version, this has the mist "receding", thus suggesting a past event, but simultaneously promising a possible future respite from the transient condition of the self on the beach, always "flowing". Thus the recession (one would normally understand, a recession into the past) is here puzzlingly a recession into the future. As a result we may see the poem as happening twice, particularly in the French version, where the end of stanza two ("qui s'ouvre et se referme") repeats that of stanza one ("et finira le jour de son commencement"), and where opening and closing is synonymous with ending and beginning. There are two countervailing impulses in the poem. One is centripetal, stressing the presentness of the self, the sense and the suffering of duration: his life both flees and pursues him, he can neither catch it nor escape from it. The other is centrifugal: there is a draining-away towards "beginning" and towards "end". Is this an attempt to reinstate a teleology? If so, we may remark further that this "beginning" and "end" are inaccessible, unknowable.

The beautiful long line "où je n'aurai plus à fouler ces longs seuils mouvants/when I may cease from treading these long shifting thresholds" (lines 8 and 7) is the climax of the poem. It suggests a breaking wave—an impression partly generated by the wave-like variation in the line-lengths, which rise from eight to thirteen syllables, then die away to five in the last line (six in the French text). This long climactic line poignantly expresses both suffering at the effort of duration (and the duration of effort) and an imagined, longed-for release. A door has only two modes, open and shut, and one precludes the other. This craving to inhabit a binary system is, of course, a Beckettian constant. It is formulated humorously in the early text *Murphy* as follows: "Humanity is a well with two buckets, one going down to be filled, the other coming up to be emptied."[12] But in spite of this and other more elaborate assertions of rational order, all of which simultaneously breathe a wry scepticism, the position of the Beckettian subject is inadequately rendered by such a dualist mathesis. In the present poem, we might see the speaker as being in a condition of Heideggerian "thrownness" upon the beach, and unable to incorporate himself into the system either of the land or of the sea. The novel *Molloy* (which, as we have seen, belongs to the same period in Beckett's work) contains a relevant passage:

> There are people the sea doesn't suit, who prefer the mountains or the plain. Personally I feel no worse there than anywhere else. Much of my life has ebbed away before this shivering expanse, to the sound of the waves in storm and calm, and the claws of the surf. Before, no, more than before, one with, spread on the sand, or in a cave. In the sand I was in my element, letting it trickle between my fingers, scooping holes that I filled in a moment later or that filled themselves in, flinging it in the air by handfuls, rolling in it. [...] And that my land went no further, in one direction at least, did not displease me. And to feel there was one direction at least in which I could go no further, without first getting wet, then drowned, was a blessing.[13]

Like Molloy, though without the air of bitter resignation, the speaker in the poem is precisely *between*: neither properly on land nor at sea, and (at least in the French version) actually composed in substance either of sand, or of the water flowing in it.[14] Hubert Dreyfus's recent commentary on Heidegger is illuminating here. Considering Heidegger's understanding of mood as all-pervasive, and how traditional philosophy has overlooked it, he stresses how mood reveals thrownness. He goes on to reiterate how for Heidegger being, or *dasein*, is "always already given" and is "a self-interpreting foundness" which Heidegger calls "thrownness". The terms Heidegger uses are strongly reminiscent of Beckett's in this poem: "This characteristic of Dasein's being—this 'that it is'—is veiled in its 'whence' and 'whither', yet disclosed in itself all the more unveiledly; we call it the *thrownness* of this entity into its 'there' [...]. The expression 'thrownness' is meant to suggest *the facticity of its being delivered over*."[15]

This condition of the inescapability, and unwilling continuance, of a painful subjectivity is, of course, one very frequently rendered in Beckett's work. Despite his ostensible dismissal of philosophical influence, Beckett's kinship with phenomenology is evident in his work—a fact which in the last decade or so has at last been receiving appropriate critical attention. The presence of phenomenological language is most evident in the early monograph on Proust, where he constantly stresses the multiplicity of selves, or "subjects" (the word is his), and emphatically rejects the understanding of the self as an essence and the empiricist notion that objects make up the phenomenal world. Throughout that essay, he concurs raptly with Proust's representation of the world as constituted by consciousness, and also of the precarious and problematic mode of existence of that consciousness.[16]

All Beckett's work simultaneously struggles for, and endlessly casts doubt on, the notion of a completed and secure selfhood; this is perhaps most evident in the splintered and deferring narrators of the trilogy.[17] In his Hegelian interpretation of the fiction, Hans-Joachim Schulz sees the protagonists as embattled Cartesians, struggling continually to preserve a humanist psychic order against the forces of disintegration. Schulz includes Beckett himself among the rearguard fighters for the rationalist Western philosophical tradition, as does Leo Bersani, who presents Beckett as the melancholy last champion of the traditional unified subject.[18] Other critics increasingly disagree, and these critics—most effectively Angela Moorjani and David Watson—discern in Beckett's definitive dismantling of fictional form a deconstructionist project *ante verbum*, since the trilogy precedes by nearly two decades the full development of post-structuralist thought.[19]

The best way to view this issue is surely to note the fierce refusal of Beckett's text to give up either position, whether that of desiring determinate meaning and a blissful arrest of deferral and duration ("cher instant je te vois"), or the conviction of actual indeterminacy and infinite semiosis ("dans ce rideau de brume qui recule"). There is a passage in *Murphy* which applies to this uncomfortable dilemma: "'The repudiation of the known,' said Neary, 'a purely intellectual operation of unspeakable difficulty'" (page 124). We leave the protagonist of this poem in his double, ceaselessly riven state, between the shingle and the dune (and French and English), forever longing for the mist to lift, and meanwhile continuing wearily to tread the thresholds of consciousness. The door at the end of the poem is a virtual door, which can be expected to open—and, which is worse, to shut—only in the realm of unfulfilled desire, that is to say, in a fiction. It is this fiction, however, which saves: a paradox held in place with that steely insistence which is Beckett's most distinctive quality.

## NOTES

1   Samuel Beckett, *Poems in English* (London, Calder and Boyars, 1961), pp. 48–49.
2   M. Frank, "The Infinite Text", translated by M. Schwerin, *Glyph*, 7 (1980), 96; quoted in A. Moorjani, *Abysmal Games in the Novels of Samuel Beckett* (Chapel Hill, University of North Carolina Department of Romance Languages, 1982), p. 131, n. 71.
3   M. Perloff, *The Poetics of Indeterminacy: Rimbaud to Cage* (Princeton, Princeton University Press, 1981), pp. 245–47. There is a brief mention in J. Fletcher, *Samuel Beckett's Art* (London, Chatto and Windus, 1967), p. 39.
4   L. Harvey, *Samuel Beckett, Poet and Critic* (Princeton, Princeton University Press, 1970), pp. 225–28. Harvey's discussion is sensitive but leans somewhat questionably on biographical data.
5   Samuel Beckett, "Peintres de l'empêchement", in *Disjecta*, edited by R. Cohn (London, Calder, 1983), pp. 133–37.
6   L. Harvey, *Samuel Beckett*, notes the, perhaps unavoidable, resolution of this suggestive ambiguity in the Italian ("seguo") and German ("ich bin") versions (p. 226).
7   It will be recalled that the "tenor" is the purport or general drift of thought regarding the subject of a metaphor, and the "vehicle" that which serves to carry or embody the tenor.
8   "I would describe men [...] as occupying in Time a much greater place than that so sparingly conceded to them in Space, a place indeed extended beyond measure, because, like giants plunged in the years, they touch at once those periods of their lives—separated by so many days—so far apart in Time": Samuel Beckett, *Proust* (London, Chatto and Windus, 1931), p. 12.
9   Samuel Beckett, *Poems in English*, p. 23. In Dante (*Purgatorio*, xxx. 22–33) the poet compares the veiled Beatrice to the rising sun shrouded in a haze.
10  See U. Eco, *A Theory of Semiotics* (Bloomington, Indiana University Press, 1976), pp. 69–72, 125–28.
11  R. Barthes, *Image Music Text*, edited and translated by S. Heath (London, Fontana, 1977), p. 147.
12  Samuel Beckett, *Murphy* [1938] (London, Calder, 1962), p. 37.
13  Samuel Beckett, *The Beckett Trilogy* (London, Picador, 1979), p. 68.
14  Harvey, I think quite mistakenly, dispels this crucial indeterminacy by literalizing the setting of the poem: "Out of [...] such a walk on Killiney beach under such characteristically Irish conditions came the present

poem" (L. Harvey, *Samuel Beckett*, p. 226). This reduction of the text by shackling it to a biographical locale also bedevils Eoin O'Brien's enterprise in his sumptuously photographed *The Beckett Country* (Dublin, Black Cat Press, 1986). See the discussion of these and related matters in my essay "'The Poetry Is Another Pair of Sleeves': Beckett, Ireland and Modernist Lyric Poetry", in *Modernism and Ireland: The Poetry of the 1930s*, edited by P. Coughlan and A. Davis (Cork, Cork University Press, 1995), pp. 173–208.

15  Martin Heidegger, *Being and Time* [1927] (Oxford, Blackwell, 1962), p. 174; quoted in H. Dreyfus, *Being-in-the-World* (Boston, MIT Press, 1992), p. 173.

16  See Samuel Beckett, *Proust*, pp. 13–19, 21, 29, 31, 47 for specific examples of these themes, which are, however, present everywhere in Beckett's discussion.

17  See P. Coughlan, "'A Noise of Wet Kisses and Washing in a Tub': Beckett's Trilogy and the Idea of Fiction", *Maynooth Review*, 6 (1980), 35–48.

18  H-J. Schulz, *This Hell of Stories: A Hegelian Approach to the Fiction of Samuel Beckett* (The Hague, Mouton, 1973), pp. 104, 106, 110; L. Bersani, *Balzac to Beckett: Center and Circumference in French Fiction* (New York, Oxford University Press, 1970), Ch. 5.

19  D. Watson, *Paradox and Desire in Samuel Beckett's Fiction* (London, Macmillan, 1991). Watson and Angela Moorjani, *Abysmal Games*, give highly suggestive and rigorous post-structuralist and psychoanalytic readings of Beckett.

# "SOMETHING OLD, SOMETHING NEW, SOMETHING BORROWED…": THE POETRY OF NUALA NÍ DHOMHNAILL AND CATHAL Ó SEARCAIGH

*Caoimhín Mac Giolla Léith*

The question of literary influence is a particularly vexed one for modern literature in Irish, principally because of the peculiar relationship this literature has with the English language and with literature in English. Modern Gaelic literature is the product of a conscious, indeed self-conscious, attempt at the end of the last century to revive a moribund tradition as part of a cultural nationalist project which inevitably and indelibly coloured the literature it produced. Moreover, since its inception many contributions to this literature have been made both by native English speakers and by native Irish speakers living and working in a predominantly English-speaking environment. It is hardly surprising then that one of the most enduring critical debates since the early years of the revival has concerned the degree to which writers in Irish have compromised or tainted their writing by an unhealthy recourse to external (specifically English-language) sources and models.

The earliest and most notable example of this was Richard Henebry's well-known attack, published in 1892, on the early poetry of the revival movement:

> Much of the body of contemporary song is worthless, much of it in such vicious taste as to be charged with untold possibilities of harm, that must debase and subvert purity of style in the future. Correct, commonplace English sentiment, thought, expression, it is, in greater part, with a miserable tortured poor shred of Irish for veneering.[1]

It is some indication of the endurance of the debate initiated by Henebry that a recent essay by Gearóid Ó Crualaoich, containing the assertion that the discourse of most modern Gaelic poetry is in fact merely the discourse of English poetry covered by a thin patina of Gaelic words and syntax, caused considerable uproar among both Gaelic poets and other critics.[2] The few poets who, in Ó Crualaoich's view, were genuinely writing within the discourse of Gaelic poetry were those who engaged in a dialogue with previous writers in the language. Yet a number of prominent modern Gaelic writers have explicitly rejected the desirability or even the possibility of such a dialogue. In 1953 Mairtín Ó Direáin, in defending his fellow poet Seán Ó Ríordáin against charges remarkably similar to those made by Henebry sixty years earlier and by Ó Crualaoich almost forty years later, asserted:

> Nár chabhair mhór don Ríordánach ná d'éinne againn san aois seo aon uaill ná mac alla ó na filí chuaigh romhainn inár dteanga féin. Tá an bhearna rómhór.[3]

> [No cry or echo from the poets who preceded us in our language would be of any help to Ó Ríordáin or to any of us in this era. The gap is too wide.]

More recently Gabriel Rosenstock has unambiguously dismissed not just modern Gaelic literature but also modern Irish literature in English as a viable background against which his own poetry might be viewed:

> 'Bhfuil dualgas ar an bhfile cur le sruth na h-éigse? Ní chuige sin atáimse. Tagann an pointe i saol an scolamáin nuair is ceart dó bailiú leis. Sa chomhthéax sin b'fhearr liom abairtín amháin de chuid Kurt Vonnegut Jnr ná gach ar scríobhadh le leathchéad bliain anuas sa traidisiún Angla-Éireannach. (Eisceacht Myles.)[4]

> [Has the poet an obligation to add to the literary tradition? That is not what I am about. There comes a point in the fledgling's life when he must fly the nest. In that context I would prefer one small sentence from Kurt Vonnegut Jnr to anything written in the last fifty years in the Anglo-Irish tradition. (Myles is an exception.)]

Yet in both these instances we might be forgiven for suspecting that these poets may be protesting too much in their attempts to shuffle off the constricting fetters of a prescriptive and parochial notion of poetic history and poetic influence. For Harold Bloom these two terms denote one and the same thing. Bloom asserts that "Poetic history [... is] indistinguishable from poetic influence, since strong poets make that history by misreading one another, so as to clear imaginative space for themselves."[5] Bloom's complex but influential model of literary influence has been much invoked and, in his view, frequently misrepresented in the past twenty years, and I mention it merely as a point of departure for a consideration of the work of two contemporaries of Rosenstock: Nuala Ní Dhomhnaill and Cathal Ó Searcaigh. While these poets have close connections with the Kerry and Donegal Gaeltachtaí respectively, they have also both spent a considerable time in an urban English-speaking environment in Dublin and abroad. The range of literary influences to which they have been subject is considerable, but what I should like to suggest is that there are some intriguing differences between their respective ways of assimilating these influences. While concentrating for the most part on a number of poems by Ní Dhomhnaill, I shall conclude with a brief look at Ó Searcaigh in order to highlight what I perceive as these divergences.

Of the various sources drawn upon in the poetry of Nuala Ní Dhomhnaill the most obvious and the most widely acknowledged is the folklore of the native Gaelic oral tradition, more specifically the folk narrative of the Dingle peninsula. Her borrowings from this source are manifest at a number of levels, from the idiomatic and stylistic to the thematic. Of course modern Gaelic poets as diverse as Máire Mhac an tSaoi and Douglas Hyde have shown a similar readiness to borrow from tradition. Yet Ní Dhomhnaill's use of such traditional material is frequently more striking and more subversive than that of her predecessors.

A number of poems may be mentioned in passing as preliminary examples. "Athchuairt ar Valparaiso" ["Return visit to Valparaiso"] (*An Dealg Droighin*, p. 51),[6] for instance, is merely the most obvious example of a poem which simultaneously repeats and explodes an antecedent text, in this instance the much anthologized "Valparaiso" by Monsignor Pádraig de Brún, a poem which became such a schoolbook classic that it is often forgotten that it was originally a translation from English. A more telling example, however, is a poem like "Oileán" ["Island"] (*Feis*, p. 14),[7] in which the ancient conceit

of a feminized landscape is inverted in an erotically charged paean to
the male body figured as the island of the poem's title. This
composition shares certain features with a number of others in which
the roles commonly assigned to male and female in patriarchal
scopophilia—that is to say, in which the woman is invariably the
object of the male gaze—are reversed: two obvious instances are the
poems "Gan do chuid éadaigh" ["Without your clothes"] (*Feis*, p.
66) and "Fear" (*Feis*, p. 64), the title of which has been suggestively
rendered by Eiléan Ní Chuilleanáin as "Looking at a man".[8] The
poem "Caitlín" (*Feis*, p. 32) pulls out all the stops to travesty the
inherited stereotype of Cathleen Ní Houlihan. This poem has, to the
best of my knowledge, not been translated. This is hardly surprising
as any English translation must inevitably obscure the fact that the
bulk of the poem comprises a hilariously overwritten and consciously
discordant *bricolage* of appropriate phrases from the poetry of Patrick
Pearse and the eighteenth-century poets Aogán Ó Rathaille and Seán
Clárach Mac Domhnaill, from the Gaelic song tradition and from
traditional proverbs.

Ní Dhomhnaill has also, however, drawn from non-Gaelic
sources. Of these the guiding lights of her early poetry are un-
questionably the sonnets of Shakespeare and the *Dream Songs* of John
Berryman. It is the latter I propose to address here. No modern Irish
poet, with the possible exception of Tom Mac Intyre, has learned
more from Berryman. The poem "Gluais leat, a scríbhinn" (*An Dealg
Droighin*, p. 30) was written in 1977 and is explicitly presented as an
"imitation of Berryman" ("aithris ar John Berryman"). It begins:

> Gluais leat, a scríbhinn, go mí-ámharúil
> is abair i gcogar léi
> nó scairt amach os ard
> (ina cluais sin amháin)
> go bhfuil sí dathúil.

Berryman's "Dream Song No. 171" likewise begins:

> Go, ill-sped book, and whisper to her or
> storm out the mention for her only ear
> that she is beautiful.[9]

Ní Dhomhnaill's is a fairly faithful translation apart from the excision
of Henry, the principal character who haunts the *Dream Songs* and is,
according to Berryman, "a white American in early middle age

sometimes in blackface, who has suffered an irreversible loss and talks to himself in the first person, sometimes in the third, sometimes even in the second".[10] The third-person references to Henry are replaced in Ní Dhomhnaill's version by references in the first person to the speaker of the poem; the gender of the object of affection remains unchanged.

Ní Dhomhnaill's appropriation of the highly idiosyncratic voice of this poem-sequence seems remarkably effortless and assured and is an early example of her prodigious ventriloquism. Yet she still manages in the poem's title and opening line to add to its resonance in Irish by invoking the opening lines of well-known epistolary poems from the sixteenth and seventeenth centuries such as "Gluais a litir, ná leig sgís" and "Mo bheannacht leat a scríbhinn".

The only other explicit reference to Berryman in Ní Dhomhnaill known to me occurs in the poem "Sionnach" ["Fox"] (*An Dealg Droighin*, p. 86), where the authority of Gottfried Benn is invoked, refracted through Berryman, only to be effectively undermined in the closing lines:

A mhaidrín rua,
rua rua rua rua
nach breá nach bhfuil fhios agat
dá mhéid a ritheann leat,
sa deireadh
gurbh é siopa an fhionnadóra
a bheidh mar chríoch ort.

Nílimidne filí
pioc difriúil.
Deir John Berryman
go ndeir Gottfried Benn
go bhfuilimid ag úsáid ár gcraiceann
mar pháipéar falla
is go mbuafar orainn.

Ach fógra do na fionnadóirí;
bígí cúramach.
Ní haon ghiorria
í seo agaibh
ach sionnach rua
anuas ón gcnoc.
Bainim snap
as láimh mo chothaithe.

> [Little red fox,
> o little red fox so red,
> how come you still don't know
> that no matter how fast you run
> the furrier's shop
> is where you'll end up?
>
> We poets
> are no different.
> John Berryman says
> that Gottfried Benn says
> that we are using our skins for wallpaper
> and that we cannot win.
>
> But a word of warning to the furriers.
> Beware.
> This is no mere hare
> you're dealing with
> but a red fox
> down from the mountain.
> I bite the hand that feeds me.][11]

While the poem opens with an echo of the Gaelic children's song "A mhaidrín rua, rua, rua, rua, rua", the second stanza refers to number 53 of the *Dream Songs*, which ends:

> Kierkegaard wanted a society, to refuse to read, papers,
> and that was not, friends, his worst idea.
> Tiny Hardy, towards the end, refused to say *anything*,
> a programme adopted early on by long Housman,
> and Gottfried Benn
> said: We are using our own skins for wallpaper and we cannot win.[12]

Given that in the previous stanza of Berryman's three-stanza poem Eliot ("the Honourable Possum") is also invoked along with an unnamed novelist (also male?), we have here a veritable chorus of the poet's world-weary buddies' gloomy musings. Ní Dhomhnaill's precise wording in Irish, however ("Deir John Berryman/go ndeir Gottfried Benn/go [...]"), obliquely echoes the traditional formula "Dúirt bean liom go ndúirt bean léi" ["A woman told me that a woman told her]", with its implied, patronizing caricature of the female gossip. This is especially intriguing in a poem the closing lines of which suggest that the ungrateful oppressed may not always be as powerless as they seem.

While these are the only overt borrowings from Berryman, other echoes of him abound in Ní Dhomhnaill's work. The hitherto untranslated "An Lá San" ["That Day"] (*An Dealg Droighin*, p. 35) begins:

> Is an lá san
> do luigh rud ar mo chroí
> chomh trom san
> dá mbeadh céad bliain is breis agam
> á ghlanadh as mo chuimhne
> ní fhéadfainn é [...],

> [And that day
> something lay on my heart
> so heavy
> that if I had a hundred years and more
> to erase it from my mind
> I could not manage it (...)],

which, before going its own way, clearly salutes "Dream Song No. 29":

> There sat down, once, a thing on Henry's heart
> so heavy, if he had a hundred years
> & more, & weeping, sleepless, in all them time
> Henry could not make good [...].[13]

More recently, and at a greater remove, the opening of "Clabhsúr" (*An Dealg Droighin*, p. 80), which could be translated as "End of story", appears to retain the memory of "Dream Song No. 77". Ní Dhomhnaill's poem begins:

> [...] is ansan,
> lá, do bhailibh an dia leis.

> D'éirigh ar maidin le fáinne an lae ghléigil,
> rug ar a rásúr, a scuab fiacal is a *thravelling bag*
> is thug dos na bonnaibh é.

> [...] and then,
> one day,
> the god just upped and left.

> Rose at the crack of dawn,
> grabbed razor, toothbrush, travelling bag
> and hit the road.]

The first stanza of Berryman's poem reads as follows:

> Seedy Henry rose up shy in de world
> & shaved & swung his barbells, duded Henry up
> and p.a.'ed poor thousands of persons on topics of grand moment
>                     to Henry, ah to those less and none.
> Wif a book of his in either hand
> he is stript down to move on.[14]

At a more general level still, the earlier short sequence of poems (*An Dealg Droighin*, pp. 15–18) on Mór of Munster, the mythological personage who in some ways resembles a female "Mad Sweeney", is also clearly indebted to the nervous, jazzy, rhythms of the Henry poems: and the frequent wry self-deprecation of the "Dream Songs" also recurs in this poem sequence.

Ní Dhomhnaill's magpie nature has not confined itself to borrowing from Berryman alone. The well-known "Táimid damanta, a dheirféaracha" (*Féar Suaithinseach*, pp. 17–18) begins:[15]

> Táimid damanta, a dheirféaracha,
> sinne a chuaigh ag snámh
> ar thránna istoíche is na réalta
> ag gáire in aonacht linn,
> an mhéarnáil inár dtimpeall
> is sinn ag scréachaíl le haoibhneas
> is le fionnuaire na taoide...

> Chaitheamar oícheanta ar bhántaibh Párthais
> ag ithe úll is spíonán is róiseanna
> laistiar dár gcluasa, ag rá amhrán
> timpeall tinte cnámh na ngadaithe,
> ag ól is ag rangás le mairnéalaigh agus robálaithe
> is táimid damanta, a dheirféaracha.

> Níor chuireamar cliath ar stoca
> níor chíoramair, níor shlámamair,
> níor thuigeamair de bhanlámhaibh
> ach an ceann atá ins na Flaithis in airde [...].

It has been translated by Michael Hartnett:

> We are damned, my sisters,
> we who swam at night
> on beaches, with the stars
> laughing with us
> phosphorescence about us
> we shrieking with delight
> with the cold of the tide...

> We spent nights in Eden's fields
> eating apples, gooseberries; roses
> behind our ears, singing songs
> around the gipsy bonfires
> drinking and romping with sailors and robbers:
> and so we're damned sisters.

> We didn't darn stockings
> we didn't comb or tease
> we knew nothing of handmaidens
> except the one in high Heaven [...].

We may compare this with Elaine Feinstein's translation of a poem originally composed in 1915 by the Russian Marina Tsvetayeva, which begins:

> We shall not escape Hell, my passionate
> sisters, we shall drink black resins—
> we who sang our praises to the Lord
> with every one of our sinews, even the finest
> we did not lean over cradles or spinning wheels at night and now
>                                                    we are
> carried off by an unsteady boat
> under the skirts of a sleeveless cloak,
> we dressed every morning in
> fine Chinese silk, and we would
> sing our paradisal songs at
> the fire of the robbers' camp,

> slovenly needlewomen (all
> our sewing came apart), dancers,
> players upon pipes: we who have been
> the queens of the whole world![16]

The mere listing of these sources and borrowings, however, can become an arid and fairly trivial exercise in literary detective work. What should interest us here is not the fact but the nature of Ní Dhomhnaill's intertextuality. In some instances, such as the Berryman imitation mentioned earlier or this unattributed reworking of Tsvetayeva, Ní Dhomhnaill seems simply to have chanced upon works which chimed intriguingly with her current concerns and to have refashioned them in Irish as a kind of literary five-finger exercise. There are, however, other, perhaps ultimately more significant, cases in which her response to a pre-existent text or texts takes the more radical form of a redress. Poems such as "Oileán" or "Caitlín", which have been mentioned already, fall into this category, as does yet another intriguing poem. The composition "An Bhean Mhídhílis" in Ní Dhomhnaill's latest collection *Feis* (pp. 70–71), though not acknowledged as such, is clearly a reply to Federico García Lorca's famous poem "La casada infiel" ["The unfaithful wife"] from the *Romancero gitano*. Lorca's poem has, as it happens, also been translated into English by Michael Hartnett and into Irish by Máire Mhac an tSaoi.[17]

The ballad in Spanish is a laconic first-person account—though one rich in quasi-surrealist metaphor—of a gipsy's night-time seduction by the river of the unfaithful wife of the poem's title, whom he initially believes to be an unwed young girl. Ní Dhomhnaill's poem gives the woman's account of a comparable, if somewhat updated and culturally transposed, encounter:

> Do phioc sé suas mé
> ag an gcúntúirt
> is tar éis beagáinín cainte
> do thairrig sé deoch dom
> nár eitíos uaidh
> is do shuíomair síos
> ag comhrá.
> Chuamair ó dheoch go deoch
> is ó *joke go joke*
> is do bhíos-sa sna trithí aige
> ach dá mhéid a bhíos ólta
> ní dúrt leis go rabhas pósta...
>
> [He picked me up
> at the counter

and, after some small talk,
offered me a drink
which I didn't refuse
and we sat down
for a chat.
We went from drink to drink
and from joke to joke
and he had me in stitches
but no matter how drunk I got
I didn't tell him I was married...]

The narrative proceeds as follows: the woman takes a lift from this man and they turn into a lay-by, the description of which is deliberately de-romanticized with the detail of ripped plastic sacks full of refuse strewn about the place, where they have sexual intercourse. In Lorca's poem it was the account of the copulation that inspired some of its most famous images:

> Sus musclos se me escapaban
> como pesces sorprendidos,
> la mitad llenos de lumbre,
> la mitad llenos de frío.

> Aquella noche corrí
> el mejor de los caminos
> montado en potra de nácar
> sin bridos sin estribos.

Michael Hartnett translates:

> Like frightened fish
> they slipped from me, her thighs:
> one full of cold,
> the other full of fire.
> On the best highway
> that night I was riding
> saddling a mare of mother-of-pearl
> without stirrups or bridle.

Nuala Ní Dhomhnaill's response to this passage is very different from Hartnett's or that of Máire Mhac an tSaoi. Ní Dhomhnaill seizes the central metaphor of the second stanza quoted and inverts the power roles literally while simultaneously offering an incidental critique of conventional marriage:

is nuair a shuíos síos air go cúramach
is gur mharcaíos thar an sprioc é
ba é an chloch ba lú ar mo phaidrín
a rá leis go rabhas pósta...

is nuair a bhíos ag tabhairt pléisiúra dhó
d'fhéach sé sa dá shúil orm
is fuaireas mothú pabhair is tuisceana
nár bhraitheas ó táim pósta...

[and when I sat down on him carefully
and rode him past the mark
the last thing on my mind was
to say that I was married...

and while I was giving him pleasure
he looked into my eyes
and I had feeling of power and understanding
I have not felt since I am married...]

In Ní Dhomhnaill's Irish the final line just quoted seems to be
shadowed by the alternative "nár bhraitheas ó pósadh mé" ["I have
not felt since I was married"], thereby slyly suggesting two com-
plementary interpretations: that the woman has not felt such power
or understanding *since* she got married and *because* of her married
state. In the following stanzas the man is subsequently overcome
with post-coital remorse, which simply confirms the woman's instincts in not telling him she is married, and she firmly resolves to
continue the deception should she meet him again socially. She ends
by addressing the reader, rhetorically asking, "Wouldn't you do the
same?"

Alan Titley has recently discussed this poem in the course of an
attack on what he perceives as the excesses of some feminist writing.[18]
Ignoring Lorca's original poem, Titley frivolously rewrites Ní
Dhomhnaill, once again from the male perspective, thereby produ-
cing a classic "What's sauce for the goose..." argument. If, he asks
rhetorically, his version might justifiably be accused of condoning an
offensively sexist objectification of the woman, why should similar
charges not be made against Ní Dhomhnaill? Titley's version begins
as follows:

Do phioc mé suas í
ag an gcúntúirt
Is tar éis beagáinín cainte
do thairg deoch di
nár eitigh sí uaim
Is do shuíomair síos ag comhrá.
Chuamair ó dheoch go deoch
is ó joke go joke
is do bhí sí sna trithí agam
ach dá mhéid a bhíos ólta
ní dúrt léi go rabhas pósta...[19]

[I picked her up
at the counter
and after some small talk
offered her a drink,
which she didn't refuse
and we sat down to chat.
We went from drink to drink
and from joke to joke
and I had her in stitches,
but no matter how drunk I got
I didn't let on I was married...]

Of course the obvious response to the "sauce for the goose" argument is that it would only be valid given an equitable distribution of
power and autonomy within a given society or social context. That
this is manifestly not the case in the fictional world assumed in Ní
Dhomhnaill's poem may be confirmed by any woman who has ever
sat alone at a bar counter or overheard a discussion of male versus
female marital infidelity. Titley's brusque dismissal of any counter-
argument based on gendered power relations comes as no surprise
given his apparent inability to recognize such relations, much less
transcend them.[20] It is this inability that prevents him from produ-
cing what he evidently sets out to produce, a true mirror-image of Ní
Dhomhnaill's poem. In Titley's version the unfaithful *husband* still
does the picking up, still buys the drinks, and still tells the jokes. All
of which suggests that Ní Dhomhnaill's occasional acts of subversion
of patriarchal literary tradition may not be as inconsequential as they
might initially appear.

Ní Dhomhnaill's dialogue with her literary antecedents, both
domestic and alien, can therefore be sometimes cordial and some-

times confrontational, sometimes overt, sometimes covert. Cathal Ó Searcaigh's, on the other hand, is more consistently cordial but covert. In fact his principal weakness may be a failure to temper and transcend appropriate material and thereby, in Bloomian terms, "create imaginative space for himself". Ó Searcaigh's attempts to harness the energies released by his exposure to an impressively wide range of modern poetry, especially during a number of years spent in Dublin and London, have been most successful in his most recent work, which has become increasingly rooted in the traditions and landscape of his native place in the Donegal Gaeltacht. Yet both before and since his return to Donegal the drive towards a firmly rooted regionalism in Ó Searcaigh's poetry has been a continuous struggle to find his own voice amid the cacophony which seems to be constantly ringing in his ears. His attempts to cope with the anxiety of a whole host of influences has on occasion resulted in a form of appropriation that might less charitably be described as outright plagiarism. His first three collections included Irish versions of poems by the Spanish poets Antonio Machado and Vincente Aleixandre, the Japanese Yoshino Horishi and Takaki Kyozo, the Pole Tymoteusz Karpowic, the Israeli Yehuda Amichai and the American Mary Oliver. In all but the last instance Ó Searcaigh's translations were apparently based on English versions of the original poems. Yet none of these translations was acknowledged as such until his fourth and most recent volume, a "Selected Poems" entitled *Suibhne*.[21]

Two other poets of whom initially unacknowledged translations were presented were the Welsh poet Ellis Jones and the Scottish Gaelic poet Ruaraidh MacThómais. Ó Searcaigh's version of Jones's *englyn* "Y Bargod" ["The Eaves"], which seems almost to have acquired the status of a modern Gaelic classic among translators and anthologists apparently unaware of the fact that it is not an original Ó Searcaigh poem, is most probably a translation from Ciarán Carson's adaptation from the original Welsh.[22] It is, however, useful briefly to consider a more recent and slightly more complex response by Ó Searcaigh to two poems by Ruaraidh MacThómais. Ó Searcaigh's poem "Caoineadh" ["Lament"] (*Suibhne*, p. 143) is a first-person narrative in which the speaker recalls an incident from his youth when he accompanied his mother in a search for a favourite pet sheep caught on a hill ledge, which subsequently dies painfully as the crows pluck out its eyes. The first stanza ends with the child in floods of tears as his mother attempts to comfort him with the promise of potato bread sandwiches upon their return. In the second stanza this becomes the vehicle for an extended metaphor the tenor of which is the imminent death of the poet's native language, Irish:

O dá ligfeadh sí liú amháin gaile—liú catha
A chuirfeadh na creachadóirí chun reatha
Ach seo í ag creathnú, seo í ag géilleadh;
Níl mo mháthair anseo le mé a shuaimhniú a thuilleadh
Is ní dhéanfaidh gealladh an phian a mhaolú.

[Oh, if only it (the language) were to let one heroic shout—a war-
                                                        cry
that would rout the plunderers
but here it is trembling, here it is yielding;
this time my mother is not here
and no promise will soothe the pain.]

A poem like this, which explicitly engages with the politics of language, seems almost anachronistic at a time when most Irish-language poetry exudes, superficially at least, a curious confidence in the conditions of its own existence. Gearóid Denvir and others have argued that the troubled interrogation by a previous generation of Gaelic writers of their decision, their right, or even their duty, to choose Irish as a medium, has since vanished and that Gaelic writers now "simply write" unselfconsciously. I have argued elsewhere that a closer reading of a number of contemporary poets reveals that the tensions necessarily produced by this decision to write in a minority language, which for many of them is a self-consciously acquired language, are simply displaced or subliminated, and retain an animating and indeed enabling role in the production of contemporary poetry in Irish.[23] Ó Searcaigh's poem, however, is especially poignant in that, paradoxically, the poet is able to produce the stricken cry of which the sheep and its metaphorical tenor, the Irish language, are incapable, only by ventriloquizing a poet writing in a language every bit as marginalized and imperilled as Irish. For Ó Searcaigh's "Caoineadh" is essentially an amalgam of two poems by MacThómais which appear on consecutive pages of the anthology *Nua-bhàrdachd Ghàidhlig: Modern Scottish Gaelic Poems* edited by Domhnall MacAmhlaigh.[24] The poem "Anns a' Bhalbh Mhadainn", translated as "Sheep", provides both the setting for Ó Searcaigh's poem and the two-stanza format of vehicle and tenor for Mac-

Thómais's extended metaphor in which the blanket of snow covering Scotland becomes a shroud. The second stanza closes the poem as follows:

> Thainig stoirm air mo dhùthaich,
> sneachda min, marbhteach, mùchaidh:
> ge geal e, na creid 'na ghilead,
> na cuir t'earbs ann an anart;
> dheanadh mo chridhe iollach
> nam faicinn air a' chlàr bhàn sin ball buidhe
> 's gun tuiginn gu robh anail a' Ghaidheil a' tighinn am mullach.

> [A storm came over my country,
> of fine, deadly, smothering snow:
> though it is white, do not believe in its whiteness,
> do not set your trust in a shroud;
> my heart would rejoice
> were I to see on that white plain a yellow spot,
> and understand that the breath of the Gael was coming to the
>                                                                   surface.]

This profoundly pessimistic contemplation of the death of his people is repeated in MacThómais's "Cisteachan-laighe" ["Coffins"], the closing line of which—"'s cha shlànaich tea no còmhradh an cràdh" ["and neither tea nor talk will heal the pain"]—also provides Ó Searcaigh with the last line of his poem.

In conclusion it may be noted that this is merely one, particularly telling, occasion where Ó Searcaigh's poetry appears troubled if not traumatized by the pressure of poetic history and the influence of powerful antecedents. Ó Searcaigh differs from Nuala Ní Dhomhnaill in that the latter is more likely to find such pressure animating and invigorating. Given this divergence between the two poets' treatment of borrowed sources it is tempting to suggest that the covert, occluded or sublimated nature of Ó Searcaigh's appropriations from a wide variety of sources may derive in part from a continuing, if unacknowledged and uncomfortable, subscription to a Modernist aesthetic and the tyranny of the Poundian complusion constantly to "make it new". Some hope for the survival of Irish-language poetry in the exacting and inclement climate of *Post*modernism may reside in Nuala Ní Dhomhnaill's apparent indifference to the fetishizing of originality which is one of Modernism's principal inheritances from Romanticism. Ní Dhomhnaill's unabashed appropriations, bold juxtapositions, belligerent subversions and evangelical recuperation of pre-existing texts suggest that, rather than measuring itself solely by the yardstick of high Modernism, her work ambitiously claims affinity with a much wider range of aesthetic practices, from the formulaic composition of the Homeric epics at the very beginning of Western literature to the most modish of Postmodern simulacra.

## NOTES

1   R. Henebry, "A Plea for Prose", *Irisleabhar na Gaedhilge*, 4 (June 1892), 143.

2   G. Ó Crualaoich, "Nuafhilíocht na Gaeilge: Dearcadh Dána", *Innti*, 10 (1986), 63–66. The most extensive response to Ó Crualaoich may be found in two articles by Gearóid Denvir: "Continuing the Link: An Aspect of Contemporary Irish Poetry", *The Irish Review*, 3 (1988), 40–54, and "D'aithle na bhFilí", *Innti*, 12 (1989), 103–19 (the latter being an extended version, in Irish, of the former).

3   Quoted in L. Prút, *Máirtín Ó Direáin, File Tréadúil* (Maynooth, An Sagart, 1982), p. 17. The debate aroused by certain unfavourable reviews of O'Ríordáin's first collection of poems, *Eireaball Spideoige* (Dublin, Sáirséal and Dill, 1952), has been well documented by Seán Ó Coileáin in *Seán Ó Ríordáin: Beatha agus Saothar* (Dublin, An Clóchomhar, 1982), pp. 234–66.

4   *Rogha an Fhile*, edited by E. Ó Tuairisc (Dublin, Goldsmith, 1974), p. 81.

5   H. Bloom, *The Anxiety of Influence* (London, Oxford University Press, 1953), p. 5.

6   Nuala Ní Dhomhnaill, *An Dealg Droighin* (Cork, Mercier Press, 1981).

7   Nuala Ní Dhomhnaill, *Feis* (Maynooth, An Sagart, 1991).

8   Eiléan Ní Chuilleanáin, in *Pharoah's Daughter* (Dublin, Gallery Press, 1990), p. 141.

9   John Berryman, *His Toy, His Dream, His Rest: 308 Dream Songs* (London, Faber, 1969), p. 100.

10  John Berryman, *His Toy, His Dream, His Rest*, p. x.

11  In this instance, and in all others unless otherwise indicated, the translation is by the present author.

12  John Berryman, *77 Dream Songs* (London, Faber, 1964), p. 60.

13  John Berryman, *77 Dream Songs*, p. 33.

14  John Berryman, *77 Dream Songs*, p. 84.

15  Nuala Ní Dhomhnaill, *Féar Suaithinseach* (Maynooth, An Sagart, 1984).

16  Marina Tsvetayeva, *Selected Poems* (London, Oxford University Press, 1986), p. 3.

17  Michael Hartnett, *Collected Poems* (Dublin, Raven Arts Press, 1986), pp. 58–59; Máire Mhac an tSaoi, *Margadh na Saoire* (Dublin, Sáirséal and Dill, 1956), pp. 68–70.

18  Alan Titley, "Mná agus Daoine", in *Leath na Spéire*, edited by E. Ó hAnluain (Dublin, An Clóchomhar, 1992), pp. 42–60.

19  Alan Titley, "Mná agus Daoine", p. 56.

20  Alan Titley, "Mná agus Daoine", p. 59.

21  Cathal Ó Searcaigh, *Suibhne* (Dublin, Coiscéim, 1987).

22  See C. Mac Giolla Léith in "More Canon Fodder" (review), *The Irish Review*, 11 (Winter 1991–92), 127–31.

23  C. Mac Giolla Léith, "Contemporary Poetry in Irish: Divided Loyalties and the Chimera of Continuity", *The Irish Review*, 6 (Spring 1989), 46–54.

24  *Nua-bhàrdachd Ghàidhlig: Modern Scottish Gaelic Poems*, edited by D. MacAmhlaigh (Edinburgh, Southside, 1976), pp. 154–57. The translations of these poems are by MacThómais himself.

# DER PARK BY BOTHO STRAUSS AND A MIDSUMMER NIGHT'S DREAM

## Hilda Smyth

Botho Strauss, born in 1944, is a well-known and highly respected dramatist and novelist. He lives in Berlin, where he has been closely associated with the "Schaubühne am Halleschen Ufer" in the capacity of director as well as playwright. The play which forms the subject of this essay, *Der Park*, was published in 1983. Strauss wrote a prologue to it in which he sheds light on the relationship between this play and Shakespeare's *A Midsummer Night's Dream*. His prologue translates as follows:

> Imagine: An efficient society, almost as far removed from the sacred as from the timeless poem (and already a little tired), succumbs to the genius of a great work of art, instead of to a myth or ideology. Viewed in this light, the characters and the plot of this new play are occupied and moved, elevated and fooled by the spirit of Shakespeare's *Midsummer Night's Dream*. And just as none of us can lead his own life, but only one that obeys thousands of supra- and subconscious preconditions, "structures", traditions, so too are those contemporary characters who appear here dependants and ideologists, subject to the magical domination of an ancient, enigmatic comedy. Like the love juice that Puck and Oberon administered to the sleeping lovers in the Athenian wood, a work of art now trickles into the senses of the characters here and adds to their confusion. Metamorphoses occur, however, to turn people, spirits and plot topsy-turvy—the *Midsummer Night's Dream* goes on and on, and no one there would have stayed awake and brought the antidote to rescue them quickly from their confusion.[1]

As Strauss himself unequivocally states, *Der Park* is pervaded by the spirit, or "Geist", of *A Midsummer Night's Dream*—a good example of an older, classical work of literature providing inspiration for a new creation. The two very different plays have many elements in common, some more obvious than others. Strauss, for example, retains the names Titania and Oberon, immediately identifiable with Shakespeare's fairy king and queen. But what prompted Strauss to trickle a work of art into the senses of his characters, and what overall effect does this have on his play?

It is clear that the German play is far from a modern translation of *A Midsummer Night's Dream*. *Der Park* is not a new version of an old tale, or a classic work superimposed on a more modern background. Just as Shakespeare himself was notorious for borrowing material from other sources, from which he then created his masterpieces, so too does Strauss transform the playful comedy into a biting critique of modern civilization. He relocates "the timeless poem", which is vaguely set in ancient Greece, in a specific time and place: the "efficient society" of the 1970s and 1980s. This undoubtedly reflects West German society, the one he is obviously most familiar with, but by analogy it could also be taken to refer to any Western civilization of the present time. Perhaps to widen the play's horizons, Helen, one of the protagonists, is half-American, and frequently lapses into English, which is often mingled with German to produce a collage-like effect: "Ach, what the fuck, I'm not such a dumb little cutie, das man dauernd herumkommandiern kann."[2]

That Strauss describes this imaginary society as "efficient" is telling. "Efficient" is in itself a neutral adjective, denoting a systematic, rational approach to life and implying a functioning, ordered society. Strauss, however, uses it differently—to qualify a society which, as he puts it in the prologue, is "almost as far removed from the sacred as from the timeless poem". What he considers to be "the sacred", and how it has become meaningless and devalued in the society depicted, form the basis of his play.

The playful atmosphere of Shakespeare's play demands a certain amount of suspended disbelief—the magic in the forest can operate only if it is perceived as being real. The audience must have an innocent readiness to accept as real a number of creatures rooted in myth and legend, and events that may be described as fantastical if not downright bizarre. Strauss, on the other hand—while not as extreme as Brecht, who saw theatre as a political and revolutionizing tool—, presents his audience with reality and hopes for a reaction. He does not incite change; on the contrary, he holds out very little hope of our being able to change, as is evident in his prologue: "None of us can lead his own life, but only one that obeys thousands of supra- and subconscious preconditions, 'structures', traditions." By allowing the "efficient society" to succumb to "the genius of a great work of art, instead of to a myth or ideology", he attempts to hold a mirror up to the audience to make us think about what has been implied— that we have already succumbed to the myth and ideology—and to promote an awareness of our lack of freedom. We are, to all intents and purposes, as blind and curtailed as the characters in *Der Park*, existing, as they do, in the realm of bad dreams.

This underlying awareness is what makes the play very different from the original "timeless poem". The bleak outlook for society and mankind in general is expressed explicitly in the prologue, where "the *Midsummer Night's Dream* goes on and on, and no one there would have stayed awake and brought the antidote to rescue them quickly from their confusion." Of Shakespeare's play Alexander Leggatt writes:

> Throughout the play we seem to be witnessing a constant process of exorcism, as forces which could threaten the safety of the comic world are called up, only to be driven away [...].The comic world of the play is very close to a darker world of passion, terror and chaos, yet the border between them, though thin, is never broken. [3]

This "darker world" is glimpsed now and again, as for example when the clowns introduce a lion into the play-within-a-play. The potential terror dissolves into hilarity, however, as the actor insists on revealing his identity before continuing with the action:

> You ladies—you whose gentle hearts do fear
> The smallest monstrous mouse that creeps on floor—
> May now, perchance, both quake and tremble here,
> When Lion rough in wildest rage doth roar
> Then know that I as Snug the joiner am
> A lion fell, nor else no lion's dam
> For if I should as lion come in strife
> Into this place, 'twere pity on my life. [4]

Strauss, however, creates a world in which the barriers are mercilessly ripped apart, letting the darker world hold sway and turning the dream into a refined, never-ending nightmare. The distorted, grotesque reflection Strauss offers of what he calls "the sacred" is fundamental to the play's nightmarish quality. Three aspects of "the sacred" which Strauss analyses and undermines in *Der Park* deserve our consideration: the "gods", love and death.

For most people, the word "sacred" is automatically associated with a god-figure. The gods, or god-like immortals, Oberon and Titania, figure strongly in both plays but for very different reasons. Shakespeare gave unlimited power to his immortal characters. Oberon, "King of Shadows",[5] is the all-powerful ruler of the night, and Titania, his queen, reigns over all things natural. Any disharmony in their world is reflected by disorder in the natural world of mortals. When they quarrel, seasons fluctuate wildly, and chaos rules:

> The spring, the summer,
> The chiding autumn, angry winter change
> Their wonted liveries, and all the mazed world
> By their increase now knows not which is which.
> And this same progeny of evils
> Comes from our debate, from our dissension.[6]

Such influence can also be more dynamic, as when Oberon, aided, abetted and occasionally hindered by his mischievous servant, Puck, manipulates the feelings of the human lovers with his magic love juice, causing them to fall in and out of love with each other with amazing rapidity. The influence, however, flows in one direction only: immortals may interfere in human affairs, and frequently do, but the reverse is not the case.

How then does Strauss represent the king and queen of fairyland? Our introduction to Titania and Oberon in *Der Park* could not be more ludicrous or undignified. Transported as they are from their fairy kingdom into the sterile modern world, their mission is to "awaken the deeply buried desires and melt frozen sobriety [...]. Then shall we be worshipped in the end."[7] They must restore sensuality and feeling to a world full of "vanity and tired coldness."[8] To carry out their mission, they hide among the bushes in the park and expose themselves to passers-by. What they perceive as a natural expression of sensuality is of course regarded as obscene by the more inhibited mortals. Basically, there is a communication barrier, a mutual inability to understand the nature of the other. After their first disastrous encounter with Helma, who screams and runs away at the sight of the two immortals exposing themselves, Titania remarks to

Oberon: "We're doing something wrong at the end [...]. They're disgusted, they yell at me! Is that desire? Is there any sensuality in them?"[9] She is at a loss to understand this peculiar human reaction, and her confusion is made the more poignant by her preliminary question to the passers-by: "Have you got the time, please?"

Strauss wrote in one of his novels, *Der Junge Mann* ["The Young Man"]:

> Time, time, time! How often the children in the street ask me for the time! [...] As if they came from a far-off civilization and were just flitting past [...]. They also ask out of uncertainty [...]. They are compelled to come briefly into contact with the stranger, if only to the extent of getting the time from him. "Can you tell me what time it is, please?"[10]

The plaintive question "Have you got the time, please?" may appear mundane, yet it masks Titania's need for intimacy, her desperate wish to establish a means of communication with beings that are totally alien to her. Moreover, she is attempting to conform to the behaviour patterns of human society, and first tries to establish contact according to the norms of that society. As she then plunges into fulfilling her mission by means of instant seduction, however, her attempt is doomed to failure. This unashamed sensuality, so natural to her, frightens the humans, who have long since surrendered feeling to logic and sunk into frozen indifference.

Titania emerges as a pathetic figure, compelled to be, as she complains to Oberon, a "monster in the bushes, a chilling apparition, punished like an immoral teacher, eternally damned to exposing herself",[11] while she pines for her fairy kingdom,

> Where the wild thyme blows,
> Where oxlips and the nodding violet grows,
> Quite overcanopied with luscious woodbine,
> With sweet muskroses and with eglantine.[12]

Her sensuality can find no outlet in this world; she suffers "locked in this skeleton".[13] In *A Midsummer Night's Dream*, Oberon punishes Titania for her infidelities by making her fall in love with Bottom, a man with an ass's head. Strauss's punishment is a more refined form of torture as Oberon decides, in order to punish her for her disobedience, which has placed their mission in jeopardy, "to calm this wild highness, and, as a shock, exile her briefly to a far-distant time".[14]

Titania, already uprooted from the home she loves, and alienated and withdrawn from the "efficient society" around her, is placed at an even greater distance and deprived of her last link with her own world, Oberon. It is a mental, not a physical, exile, but no less cruel for that. A stage direction has her "standing stiffly, and glancing around fearfully like a captured bird".[15]

While she is condemned to being an outsider, an alien, Titania's natural passion and desperate need for warmth drive her to fall in love with a bull. With the help of Cyprian, her "Daedalus", she mates with it, and therein lies her degradation. We are later shown Titania "lying on a white, blood-spattered sheet [...] with the hindquarters of a cow. [... She] crawls, slithers helplessly on the sheet. She sobs and says something like: 'Send the children away! The children shouldn't see me.'"[16] Shakespeare's proud, beautiful fairy queen has been "reduced to a bloody myth", as Oberon laments,[17] reduced to something too horrible for children's eyes to gaze on. Oberon cannot "take this charm from her sight/As I can take it with another herb", as his namesake claims to be able to do,[18] because he too is caught up in the nightmare.

Oberon does not share Titania's inability to come to terms with the human world; indeed he falls progressively under the influence exerted by this strange culture. He berates Titania for spreading "vanity and tired coldness", yet punishes her because she "destroys the appearance and cracks open our radiance, wherein alone our power lies".[19] His own vanity and craving for power and glory prompt him to punish Titania by means of a magic amulet crafted by Cyprian, his servant. Unknown to him, Cyprian then mass-produces these magic talismans and sells them to the mortals. When Oberon sees the results of the destructive power he has unwittingly unleashed not only on Titania but also on human couples, he is dismayed. He eschews his immortal self and the powers it commanded, for "my power, my fame are empty, my face as flat and common as a paper mask, thrown away by a happy child, now drifting in the dust at the mercy of the wind",[20] and resolves to mix with mortals. The transformation from god to mortal is perhaps most striking in the scene entitled "Seinesgleichen" ["His Kind", or "People like Him"], one of the very few scenes in the play which have titles. Oberon takes refuge with two mortals identical in appearance to himself, and Titania tries to identify her husband in the trio. So well has he physically integrated into the human world, however, that she cannot distinguish him from his counterparts. Perhaps more importantly, the two mortals are not even aware of the fact that he is different as he passes for one of them.

But is the transition from immortal to mortal really successful? Oberon chooses a false name for himself—Mittentzwei, which literally means "right in two" or "clean through the middle". As the name suggests, Oberon is in a limbo, caught between two levels, two selves: no longer a god, he cannot fully become a mortal. He is ignored by the very people he seeks to imitate: "He introduces himself—*Mittentzwei*. But no one pays any attention to him. He speaks too quietly [...]. He enters again later, once again to no avail. It's no use. They don't hear me. They don't notice me."[21] Oberon/Mittentzwei is unable to control the situation in which he finds himself and has no antidote to counteract the others' indifference, no power to attract their attention. In fact his existence gains strength only when reiterated by Erstling, a minor character who acts almost as a mouthpiece:

OBERON/MITTENTZWEI  If only it were green sauce.
WOLF  Sorry?
ERSTLING  If only it were green sauce![22]

Unable to achieve full mortal status, Oberon is also unable to resume his role as a god. This is best illustrated by his unavailing attempt to quote the famous speech of Oberon in *A Midsummer's Night Dream* which he himself quoted earlier in the play: "I know a bank where thyme blows. Cowslips. Where... Where..."[23]

Oberon and Titania, once proud gods, have been stripped of their powers and glory, and are now revealed as helpless, pathetic creatures. A final touch of irony is provided by Titania when she says, "Only a god can save us now."[24] The audience, having experienced the systematic undermining of the immortals, can find no comfort in the idea of godly salvation.

Love is another aspect of "the sacred" that is subjected to the cold, cynical reasoning of the "efficient society". Helen is loved both by her husband Georg and by his best friend, Wolf. Helma, Wolf's wife, remains on the outside, suffering from unrequited love for her husband, until the triangle is reversed by the influence of the magic talisman created by Oberon. The sequence of events is similar to the plot of *A Midsummer Night's Dream*, where Helena, Lysander, Hermia and Demetrius are subjected to immortal interference.

Strauss's play, however, evinces a considerably more jaundiced view of love.

Wolf remarks to Helen that "in the eyes and particularly in the arms of a husband, the value of his wife—let's think of the heart as a stock exchange—is in direct proportion to the attraction she holds for his best friend"; to which Helen replies, "Would you also have found me desirable if you had met me alone, not accompanied by Georg?" The answer? "Hardly."[25] Love is viewed as a possession which has no intrinsic value—it is worthwhile only when sought after by another. Georg reduces it even further when he talks about the "logic of emotions": "if everything is OK between you and him, and everything is OK between me and him, then according to the logic of emotions, everything between you and me..."[26] Love here acquires the quality of a mathematical proposition: $A = C$ and $B = C$, therefore $A$ must equal $B$. The "efficient society" imposes logic on love, the most illogical of all emotions.

The relationship between Georg and Helen is obviously based on physical attraction. He marries her because she is exotic: not only is she half-American, she is also an amateur circus trapeze artist. Their "love" has no deep foundation, as becomes all too apparent when the magic wears off and Helen refuses to sleep with him, saying: "This bag of a body is something you'd better not touch."[27] He in turn refuses to have her in his house: "If you won't swear to me that I can have you when and where I want" are the words he uses to dismiss her.[28] Here even sex, the time-honoured stand-by, is dispensed with.

Helma does seem to love Wolf, but again their relationship is not ideal. Helma herself is aware of the brittle foundations of their relative contentment when she says: "A *vis-à-vis* would be the end. Irrevocably."[29] Under the influence of the magic talisman she wears, Wolf protests his love for her—if one can call it that. Passion it certainly is not. "She's easy to get on with," he comments; "I'm tired of searching."[30] Love, or any deep emotion, is portrayed as lukewarm at best, cruelly distorted at worst.

The third aspect of "the sacred" that Strauss sets out to undermine is death. In *Der Park* we are treated to a depiction of death as viewed by a sophisticated, rational society. It is personified as a man in black, who visits Helen. Her reaction, far from being fearful, is rather one of curiosity. She asks him: "Do you want to warn me? Do you want me to lead a better life? [...] You are death. You have the power." He replies: "I don't believe in it" and giggles.[31] Strauss adopts an archetypal figure, traditionally feared and respected, and turns him into a clown who laughs, a helpless bogeyman who is exposed as a fake. Death, the final chapter in our lives, is deflated. At the end of *A Midsummer Night's Dream* Puck reminds us, "You have but slumbered here/While these visions did appear."[32] The dream element in the title is thereby reinforced. Strauss, on the other hand, links his epilogue to his prologue. The epilogue is spoken by Titania's son, the offspring of her tempestuous mating with the bull, and is set twenty-five years further on. The occasion is Titania's silver wedding anniversary, but her son maintains: "[It's] just like every other day. And the little bit that's not like every other day, that's just like every other Tuesday [...]. This Tuesday shouldn't have turned out like every other Tuesday in the long history of Tuesdays."[33] The characters in the play, and by implication today's society, are doomed to an eternal repetition of Tuesdays; there is no escape from the bleak life of every day. Here, the midsummer night's nightmare goes on and on to infinity, and no one stays awake to administer the antidote. Strauss has presented us with a rather grim, and in parts grotesque, view of modern life and society. Yet although the play seems to offer no hope of salvation for its characters, it could be seen in a more hopeful light. *Der Park* attempts to open our eyes and awaken our consciousness, and therefore may itself be regarded as an antidote to the unease and indifference that often characterize various aspects of contemporary Western civilization.

## NOTES

1  Botho Strauss, *Der Park* (Munich–Vienna, Hanser, 1984), p. 7.

2  Botho Strauss, *Der Park*, p. 10.

3  A. Leggatt, *Shakespeare's Comedy of Love* (London, Methuen, 1974), p. 23.

4  William Shakespeare, *A Midsummer Night's Dream*, edited by S. Wells (Harmondsworth, Penguin, 1967), v. 1. 215–22.

5  William Shakespeare, *A Midsummer Night's Dream*, iii. 2. 357.

6  William Shakespeare, *A Midsummer Night's Dream*, ii. 1. 111–16.

7  Botho Strauss, *Der Park*, p. 16.

8  Botho Strauss, *Der Park*, p. 11.

9  Botho Strauss, *Der Park*, p. 15.

10  Botho Strauss, *Der Junge Mann* (Munich–Vienna, Hanser, 1984), p. 1.
11  Botho Strauss, *Der Park*, p. 16.
12  William Shakespeare, *A Midsummer Night's Dream*, II. 1. 249–52.
13  Botho Strauss, *Der Park*, p. 19.
14  Botho Strauss, *Der Park*, p. 35.
15  Botho Strauss, *Der Park*, p. 39.
16  Botho Strauss, *Der Park*, p. 80.
17  Botho Strauss, *Der Park*, p. 82.
18  William Shakespeare, *A Midsummer Night's Dream*, II. 1. 183–84.
19  Botho Strauss, *Der Park*, p. 20.
20  Botho Strauss, *Der Park*, p. 94.
21  Botho Strauss, *Der Park*, p. 89.
22  Botho Strauss, *Der Park*, p. 114.
23  Botho Strauss, *Der Park*, p. 113.
24  Botho Strauss, *Der Park*, p. 119.
25  Botho Strauss, *Der Park*, p. 29.
26  Botho Strauss, *Der Park*, p. 30.
27  Botho Strauss, *Der Park*, p. 118.
28  Botho Strauss, *Der Park*, p. 118.
29  Botho Strauss, *Der Park*, p. 90.
30  Botho Strauss, *Der Park*, p. 76.
31  Botho Strauss, *Der Park*, p. 95.
32  William Shakespeare, *A Midsummer Night's Dream*, V. 1. 415–16.
33  Botho Strauss, *Der Park*, p. 127.

# SHOULD WE FORGET
# THE EUROPEAN TRADITION?

*Marella Buckley*

When Paul Valéry wrote *Crisis of the Mind* in 1921, he launched the European tradition into a new line of enquiry. Valéry was querying our identity as Europeans and asked where we had gone wrong. Writing after the "war to end all wars", he could not have known that he was pointing us down a new path that people like Benjamin, June, Steiner, Kristeva and Miller would have to take again: sadly, their enquiries have had to punctuate our century.

In trying to grasp Europe's reaction to the War, Valéry reached for the simplest metaphor available, the image of the traumatized organism or self. And he found that in order to speak of this "agonie de l'âme européenne",[1] the "agony of the European soul", he had first to find out who Europe was. When trauma strikes consciousness it brings with it a brutal existential awakening, and the self awakens into the nightmare of its own life.

For me, enquiries like that of Valéry, embodying a *concern* which crosses disciplines and national or linguistic frontiers, are a very precious part of our European tradition. These enquiries ignore the barriers that we like to pretend exist between our inner and outer worlds. They know and show that our planet is a macrocosm of ourselves. They try to "fly higher" in order to view the spirit of the time. It is hard to situate the present in the history of ideas that it is then very easy to teach a hundred years down the road. Firstly, however, we shall be dead before future generations can tell us what is happening to us now, and secondly, they will hold us responsible for what happened and for the world they will have inherited from us.

So while we teach probing and multi-layered versions of past movements of thought, we often seem to accept for our own time a lot of official answers from that newly minted public discourse that society passes around. In an information culture like ours, where for the first time in history information is the number one product in the market-place, it is hard to know where to aim your questions. Another dilemma is the choice of discipline or ideology by which to rise vertically to get an overview of the terrain, because the land below looks different depending on the balloon in which you go up. But this is the challenge which the university poses to society, and we do not just take in the public discourse. We are paid not to generate or disseminate information (the politicians and the mass media do that) but to form ways of questioning.

Just thirty years after Valéry, Steiner had to take up the same mode of questioning again—how was Europe feeling after the Second World War? In the absence of a healing discourse, Europe had internalized and re-enacted its trauma, this time plunging deep into self-annihilation. How was this trauma to be articulated? The new European truth was a forum of horror where no intact speaking self could go. After the Second World War the European intelligentsia huddled in a wilderness outside the gates of the city, the citadel, that concept on which Europe had founded its intellectual and metropolitan life. Who could go back in there, now that the trance had ended in this second and worse awakening? All speech would have to be left at the gate. What were the intellectuals, the professionals of language, to do?

Many of those who were accustomed to making art with words faced into this awful corner of the European self. But the new truth could not be caught with words; words and this horror could not co-exist. Writers like Günter Grass, Samuel Beckett and Marguerite Duras introduced a new aesthetic of the unspeakable, framing a new literature around nothing, around the absence of an adequate means of seeing or way to think.

But there are always plenty of people around, usually among the other professionals of language—the politicians, the journalists, the academics, and even the psychoanalysts—, to set up a new camp at a little distance from the old city gates and lay plans, like the *Lord of the Flies*, to build a new city with shiny, brand-new words, words like bricks and mortar, while also denying that the old city still stands and smokes and smells of the flesh of their own family and of parts of themselves. It is because language and this horror cannot co-exist that a nimbus of brave new words can work for a while in making the horror seem to disappear. The speaker's own discourse can dance around him and mercifully beguile his eyes. Such a speaker is unable to see the old city any more. But the word-artists have always known that words can never be clean and new. The words of our various European languages had spoken unrepeatable things: simple orders in simple words. Were the writers now to suck these words clean for re-use?

The survivors lived out a nauseous dilemma: to speak in anger and hatred against anything is to stand among the angry and the hateful. So those called upon to react found themselves in an endless wrangle, an almost fascinated passion, with the dominators, while the millions who had died quietly filed ghostly and silent to their deaths. Inside themselves the mourners forever met the killers while serenity and the children filed past and could not hear them when they called.

*The Tin Drum* by Günter Grass is a book that faces directly into this post-war panic in language. Its hero refuses the middle ground of speech and aligns himself with screaming and silence, those two poles or extremities at either side of talk. Oskar turns a speechless face to the world around him, feigning what he calls a "psychic emigration",[2] pretending neither to understand nor to be capable of words. He covers his inner life with a silence that is rent only by the screams that are his his gift to the world; and Oskar's screams can shatter things.

It is very hard to answer when we ask where all the death came from and where all the selves went to. At one indisputable level (perhaps the only one) the death came out of bullets, grenades, chemicals and bombs. Matter took breath away and shattered selves. In *The Tin Drum* the hero does not talk for anyone, but his voice, his breath, shatters things. In order to salvage a part of his human-ness, Oskar must diminish: he retreats and takes a stand with his scream and his little tin drum, because "no other weapon was available."[3]

The drum, at once diary and public address system, plays both inwards and outwards. Usurping language, the drum not only conveys information, it is also the only true source. Because it speaks to and of the deeper self, like a crystal ball reflecting the self, it is a medium of genuine self-seeing and so never lies. Awakener of anarchic feelings, the drum calls out asymmetries that dismantle the fixed structures of fascism.

Oskar uses the drum to write the memoirs he is composing throughout the book. The drum functions as a historical and personal archive, on which Oskar draws to write the memoirs that constitute the novel. It is encyclopaedic and can conjure up the past as it really was. The drum colonizes the functions that we relegate to the stenograph, the word-processor, the dictaphone, the answering machine, the fax machine, the filofax—in short, those things from which we seek truth and accuracy for our own words. But here words are washed away like so much dirt on the tide of true visions that the drum can conjure up.

Although this wiping of words occurs in a novel, any novel-writing that goes on is ascribed to Oskar. He is allowed to write in the asylum (perhaps only a madman would attempt book-writing now), and *The Tin Drum* that we are reading is supposedly Oskar's production, while the author's will to words is officially severed and his hand seemingly never appears in the book. But if Grass's compositional will is obscured, Oskar's struggle with language in "this vast verbal effort" is not.[4] Naming is problematized throughout the book. Namings are seen as arbitrary and interchangeable strat-egies, as a bottomless bag of possible solutions, the truth in words being that there is no final solution: there can be no last word. Oskar's language models itself on his jazz improvisations: his discourse always takes the long way round, favouring the "tortuous and the labyrinthine".[5] He caresses notions, juggles terms, stretches phrases into elaborate patterns, and in this way preserves within incantation some tatters of the human-ness which has been expelled from the symmetries of rational speech.

For the Czech novelist Milan Kundera, the novel is "nothing other than the investigation of forgotten being".[6] "The spirit of the novel," he says, "cannot live at peace with the spirit of our time [...], a whirlpool of reduction where social life is reduced to political struggle and that in turn to the confrontation of just two great global powers."[7] Both Grass and Kundera realize that public and private are entangled with each other: in their books, effects percolate inwards and outwards through the concentric circles of society.

Kundera offers his novels as investigations that are impossible in real life, where we circulate horizontally, only guessing at each others' inner landscapes by means of the signs we exchange. Here the reader sits above with the omniscient narrator, who lifts the lids on the heads interacting below. Saussure highlighted the arbitrary sense that we fix into words in order to talk to each other. Kundera's way of seeing also revolves around the lexical. It is about meaning and the way we all experience words differently. In *The Unbearable Lightness of Being* Kundera puts in place a few centre-pieces—concepts like the body, freedom, fidelity—, and four characters waltz around them viewing them through that unique fabric woven from their experience, the elaborate lace-work of their own lives. No two characters see the same things: as they circle around these notions and cross each others' lives, they are viewing entirely different things. They cannot even know this about each other, nor can they ever glimpse each others' versions. In life we cannot see inside each others' heads, but the novel that has an omniscient narrator is larger than life.

At the centre of the book, Kundera places a "Dictionary of Misunderstood Words", in which he demonstrates how a handful of terms mean irremediably different things to Sabina and Franz. This mirrors the essay "Sixty-three Words", a dictionary of what he understands by some of his favourite terms, published in *The Art of the Novel*, that is to say, outside his fictional work. Kundera launches Saussure's model inwards towards that sanctuary where the individual keeps a unique and incommunicable dictionary, where the psychoanalyst and the omniscient novelist, but rarely the naked self and never the other, can go.

Franz, like the lonely man grabbing drinks from a tray at a party, grabs the public discourse as it passes. He inherits meanings from his society—terms and notions like notes and coins. Nourished by his institutions (his family, his social class, his profession as an academic), he seems to suckle blindly like a nursling on the language and concepts he receives. Franz thus serves the conservative impulse in society, in that, like the man in the Bible who buried his talents, he hands it all back the way he got it.

Tomas, famous surgeon and Casanova, must penetrate the surface of things; he cannot co-exist with intact surfaces, with the smooth skins of signs. Armed with his scalpel and his penis, a latter-day Don Juan, he charges through this world of façades and screens. Tomas's world is full of veils to be rent: he charges to reassure himself that there is nothing behind him, nothing heavy, nothing lastingly meaningful, nothing real. Behind everything, he finds only other people's meanings, and his life remains light.

Tereza finds herself in a different world. The arena offered to her experience is a small life locked inside a brutal family, an arena whose versions of woman, freedom, work and body constitute for her an unbearably smothering void. One day Tomas passes through the life of Tereza the waitress, a nobody in her own world. Tereza sees the bird of chance passing and grabs the rest of her life out of the air as it is flying by. With sheer compositional will, she weaves up the few inconsequential coincidences that bring her to Tomas's table on that day, and presents them to him. These are the first signs he, to whom even paternity is light and meaningless, has ever encountered that are weighty, that he is unable to pass through to nothingness, because behind these flimsy hieroglyphs stands Tereza with her suitcase and her need for life.

Valéry and Steiner asked what Europe was. Grass wrote in reaction to who Europe turned out to be. And Kundera believes that by writing novels he is working within a genre which is specifically European both in form and in spirit. Originating in the European vernaculars of the Middle Ages and shaping itself across the Enlightenment, the novel is for Kundera "incompatible with the totalitarian universe [because] the world of one single Truth and the relative, ambiguous world of the novel are moulded of entirely different substances."[8]

Sabina, Tereza and Tomas face into the infinite differing of persons. They live it instead of passing it on like an unopened present as Franz does. And we know by now how our fears are passed on unconsciously to amplify across generations like an electric current running through a human chain. History has shown us that as the sense of an unarticulated and unresolved public distress grows like a cancer, the public discourse will tighten like a belt. This is how fascism works. Its language has a shameful function: it acts like a fire-blanket or a bandage to our own wound and helps us transfer that wound onto someone else. Kundera, however, makes the dictionary a means to, and not a flight from, the complexity of being.

He is right about the novel's potential for truths fuller than those which public language can accommodate. The spirit of the European novel crossed this century at least eighty years ahead of corresponding social and political institutions. The past few years, however, have seen the manifestation in politics of a value that was nurtured at the heart of the European literary tradition from the turn of the century onwards.

Although for Valéry, and people like him, Europe has always been "le cerveau", the brain of the world,[9] a glance at its history shows it also to have been the planet's organ of phallocentric expansion. To look back either two hundred or two thousand years and watch Europe behave is to see it swell in periodic inflations where its sense of itself spills over to colour the map. Until now this intermittent eruption, ideologized as an overflow of innate vitality, has always been valorized by the European public mind. Even in the wake of Hiroshima, those who took no pleasure in it could only disapprove. International relations admitted as yet no other model to valorize.

But, as Hans Enzensberger points out in *Granta*'s special edition on the New Europe, the dawn of the twentieth century had long since seen "the end of the literary hero whose principal preoccupations were conquest, triumph and delusions of grandeur".[10] Europe's modern literary heroes have been "specialists of denial [...] representing renunciation, reduction and dismantling".[11]

To review the behaviour of our century's literary heroes across Joyce, Dostoevsky, Proust, Mann, Hesse, Kafka and many others is to reel from inadequacy to introspection at the beginning and on to mental aberration and incarceration later on. Falling down towards truths, these are purely novelistic heroes and there is no place for them on the upper crust of language. Only by reading the literature will you hear from them, because to society they turn a blank and diminished face.

In 1989, this literary consciousness of Europe suddenly manifested itself in flashes of unprecedented political action. *Granta* declared that "the real hero of deconstruction is Gorbachov, the greatest proponent of the politics of retreat."[12] The dismantling of the Soviet empire got under way while the continent appeared to initiate planetary disarmament. With the fall of the Berlin Wall Europe took a deep breath, preparing to dissolve all its internal barriers.

Europe's literary self was offering to its political face a new model of virile bravery that may save the lives of many through its ability to back down. Are there ten, twenty or thirty years left to save the world? And are we fostering the spirit of Europe's literary anti-hero, so new to the public eye? Are we breaking outmoded and dangerous structures in disarmament and in ecology, or are we inflating again the balloons of deadly heroisms? Is the New Europe, so named on the five-hundredth anniversary of Columbus's "discovery" and "exploration", proud or ashamed of what he did in our name?

The public discourse sent from the United States speaks of a "New World Order", to which our continent replies that we have a

"New Europe". Could this public discourse be a gloss over the reality of young Europeans' lives today? Is language being used once more to ward things off?

Maybe the sense of an ending into which younger Europeans have grown up is honestly invisible to those over thirty. Or perhaps we are viewing here the gap between what we carry inside us and what we have a discourse to express. Sociologists tell us that those born in the Sixties had nightmares as adolescents about the nuclear holocaust. When this sense of an imminent end was dismantled in the late Eighties, we were taking down a shroud to find a tomb behind it, and we were told that our environment would be uninhabitable before our old age. These are different types of endings. The nuclear nightmares of the Seventies were all about red buttons and red telephones: would Big Brother punish the world or would he not? But maybe this Brother would be assassinated, or overthrown in a coup; or perhaps Superman would stop him.

The mechanism of the environmental holocaust, however, is already under way. And it is not Big Brother but each of us who is causing it, merely by the way we were taught to live. Raised as little Platos and Cartesians on empiricism, rationalism, hierarchies, dualism and models of linear progress, we children of the European tradition now find that the institutions and philosophies which reared us have apparently been helping to end the world since long before we were born. We urgently need means to express this hitherto unprecedented relationship of a generation to its source. Or are we to stand by and let Europe's new fascism offer the only voice to this pain? Luckily, many of us now find in other traditions modes of research which fill in the holes in our own. And in the New World, love has become a virus with which we are killing each other. We do not even have language for this area of our experience, for endings that dissolve into larger and different endings, for birth into a dying world, for this relationship of ours to the tradition that fathered us. But a discourse will have to be found for this trouble in the family.

Outside the institutions, young people are forging such a discourse in their music, which is now a theatre of cruelty like the one Artaud called for in the Thirties (a time very like our own). Are they the only ones forging new symbolic means for the spirit of our age? There is a hole in the discourse we are sharing just like the hole we have made in the sky above. Writing from Paris on the front page of *The Guardian*, John Berger recognized this: "Between the experience of living a normal life on the planet at the moment and the public narrative being offered to give a sense to that life, the empty space—the gap—is enormous. This is why a third of the French population are ready to listen to Le Pen."[13]

Grass has stated that he writes against a tide of forgetting, what Steiner called "the creative amnesia" that swept over Europe after the Second World War.[14] And Kundera has said that he writes against a "forgetting of being" that he sees as the spirit of this age.[15] Berger put the problem very clearly in *The Guardian*. Both in the black faces of the Parisians riding the Métro alongside him and in the international behaviour that is currently reshaping our world, he sees the same symptom, "a refusal to focus on what is near" and the deadening of "that special form of attention" that is full of being.[16]

So what should Europe be forgetting? Even our tradition has realized that there is no such thing as forgetting. Freud told us that Mind, the deep self, remembers everything. Recently we have realized, to our dismay, that matter always remembers too. The planet that sustains us is suddenly appearing as a larger single mind, like an unconscious on the outside, like the omniscient God of our first confessions.

For Grass and Kundera, the opposite of forgetting is seeing. Their works catch within themselves society's taboo on full seeing, and their characters infringe it. In *The Tin Drum*, Mama's stare clings forever to the severed horse's head that is retrieved from the sea. From King Arthur to Freud, it is an ancient European notion that things, especially parts of heads, discarded in deep waters will eventually bob to the surface again. Meanwhile, in *The Unbearable Lightness of Being*, Tomas and Sabina inherit that space of play which is the European libertine tradition: they exult in sex-play with mirrors, in full seeing, while Franz will only make love with his eyes closed.

For me the opposite of forgetting is letting things be. To admit that things are in being alongside us or inside us seems somehow to loosen the hold they have over us, while avoiding things, denying them their actuality, seems only to make us shrink. Of course forgetting is impossible and we are unable to dissolve or eject what still lives for us. We can merely pretend to ourselves and to others that we are only part of what we really are. We are not urging Europe to "remember" anything. The past does not exist. What no longer is has already evaporated from our sense of things. If Auschwitz and

Hiroshima really are not a part of us and the things we do now, then let them go. We know so little anyway about the people who went into the graves of the past. But we seem at present to be finding their graves inside us. Do we leave them alone or do we allow them to *be* and let them yield up whatever of them still lives in us?

If we are to stop forgetting and let the different parts of ourselves be again, it is too late for blame to do any good. The European attitude, wherever in the world it manifests itself, must simply be seen wholly, for both its strengths and its incapacities. This attitude, which is of Greek, Roman and Judaeo-Christian origin, is a very particular way of dealing with the world. Like a goldfish in water, we may have become too familiar with our own element to perceive it and to perceive that a universe lies outside it. Our tradition seems to specialize in separation. It studies things separately and educates selected parts of the self at any one time. A Western education might be the best in the world if it included a process whereby, unlike Humpty Dumpty, one could put oneself back together again. But most people do not. And such people run our world in bits and pieces. When they operate in public, these people banish what they know from their private lives, and when they set about organizing their society they banish the attitudes they met in the arts they claim to revere. They behave as if their sense of their inner self had nothing to do with the state of the world.

Although we sometimes have cause to be ashamed of the European tradition and have reproached it for the limits of what it has offered us, it may always be our family. It offers a forum of intimacy, a sense that for better or for worse these people formed us. And the amount of forgetting that we Europeans do in the near future will decide whether the 1990s will subsequently be seen as an end or a prelude to a new beginning.

## NOTES

1    Paul Valéry, "Crise de l'esprit", in his *Œuvres*, edited by J. Hytier (Paris, Gallimard, 1957), p. 990.
2    Günter Grass, *The Tin Drum* (London, Penguin, 1965), p. 117.
3    Günter Grass, *The Tin Drum*, p. 61.
4    Günter Grass, *The Tin Drum*, p. 173.
5    Günter Grass, *The Tin Drum*, p. 45.

6   Milan Kundera, *The Art of the Novel* (London, Faber, 1988), p. 5.
7   Milan Kundera, *The Art of the Novel*, p. 17.
8   Milan Kundera, *The Art of the Novel*, p. 14.
9   Paul Valéry, "Crise de l'esprit", p. 995.
10  H. Enzensberger, *New Europe* = *Granta* [Cambridge], 30 (Winter 1990), p. 136.
11  H. Enzensberger, *New Europe*, p. 136.
12  H. Enzensberger, *New Europe*, p. 140.
13  J. Berger, in *The Guardian*, 4 Dec. 1991, p. 1.
14  G. Steiner, *In Bluebeard's Castle* (London–New Haven, Yale University Press, 1971), p. 59.
15  Milan Kundera, *The Art of the Novel*, p. 5.
16  J. Berger, in *The Guardian*, 4 Dec. 1991, p. 1.

# INDEX OF NAMES

An asterisk (*) before an entry indicates a character in mythology or literature.